Zanna

IF YOU DON'T KNOW ME BY NOW

THE OFFICIAL STORY OF SIMPLY RED
BY BRIAN SOUTHALL WITH MICK HUCKNALL

CARLTON
BOOKS

This is a Carlton/Dream Productions book.

First published in Great Britain by Carlton
Books Limited 2007, 20 Mortimer Street,
London W1T 3JW.

Artwork, Design (including cover design),
Logo and Text © Dream Productions.

A CIP catalogue for this book is available
from the British Library.

ISBN HB: 978-1-84442-442-9
ISBN PB:⋅1-84442-594-0

Writers: Brian Southall with Mick Hucknall.
Art Direction & Design: Stuart Crouch &
Melanie Hunter at Peacock. Production:
Alex Noyes & Elaine Gwyther. Executive
Editors: Andy Dodd & Ian Grenfell.

CARLTON
BOOKS

CONTENTS

INTRODUCTION

When we started out way back in 1984, I had no idea I'd ever get this far although I always had a feeling that I'd still have music as a profession 20 years on. But when you look around, there are so few bands and artists that actually stay around at this kind of level for that length of time, and I never really imagined that I'd be one of them.

I didn't know whether Simply Red would still be together or whether I'd have gone off on a solo career – I had no idea. All I did have then, and it's something I still carry with me today, is a fundamental love of music. I need to write and come up with ideas and I'll only stop when those ideas dry up... it's the only thing that drives me.

In the early days having hit records was the only guide we had to being successful and the first sense of having 'made it' was when we reached number one in America with 'Holding Back The Years'. *Stars* was the obvious high point in popularity but I rank *Home* as another high point and the new album is a continuation of that work and might even end up being my greatest moment.

Home and *Stay* are both signs of where we are going and rest assured we are nowhere near the end of Simply Red!

QUOTES

"There are no such things as part time friends and throughout the time I've known Mick, he has given me his total support and loyalty."

SIR ALEX FERGUSON

"Mick is a great vocalist – that much is obvious. He's a great interpreter of songs with performances, live and recorded, which will stand the test of time. But, in a way, this talent masks his skills as a writer. As fans of Simply Red know, he is responsible for most of their back catalogue.

I've been lucky to know Mick not just as a musician but as a loyal friend and a Labour Party supporter. What impresses me about him is that while his music has brought him great rewards, he has never forgotten his roots or values. I can vouch for the fact that his passion for politics and social justice at home and abroad is genuine as is his attachment to the Labour Party.

Mick has had a long career now. Longevity is a rare thing in pop, just as it is in politics. The key to continued success is can you find a new audience and can you get your existing audience to grow with you? It's something musicians and politicians both have to attempt. Mick has managed it better than most. He's just a really decent guy."

RT HON TONY BLAIR MP

"To Mick Hucknall – all the best wishes to a real philanthropist."

NELSON MANDELA

"Mick Hucknall is a major talent in the world of popular music. As a singer he is blessed with a truly inspiring voice which, coupled with his talent as a song-writer, and the great skill of his hot band Simply Red, has quite rightly kept him at the very top of our profession for well over two decades. This includes a memorable concert we shared together at Montreux in 1991."

QUINCY JONES

"Simply Red right? I love that album Picture Book man."

MILES DAVIS

"I've never heard anyone as good as Otis Redding or Sam Cooke. We braved the crowds to see Simply Red the other night and they were really good. What a blast – Mick you were terrific, we had a ball."

ROD STEWART

"The first thing I would say is that Mick Hucknall is one of the greatest British singers. There are lots of different things he can sing and that's the mark of a great singer. Often when you hear him sing, you'll hear a song – and it might be a song you didn't know or like – but once you hear him sing it, you like the song and that's the mark of a really great singer.

Mick also has a huge knowledge of music and has great awareness of jazz, blues, soul and popular songs.

George Harrison always said to me that he really liked Mick's voice because he always sang really nice songs and just had a beautiful voice. He can sing songs and bring them to life.

I was looking through a box of tapes of all the old Tube television programmes from the early 80s and it was interesting to see who is still around and the truth of it is that 80% of the people who are around we don't hear of anymore. To stay on in music for a long time is a very hard thing to do and the only way it can be achieved is if you are very talented and have a real gift for music which Mick has."

JOOLS HOLLAND

"Mick Hucknall produces great R&B and soul ballads. He is one of the few British musicians still keeping the soul tradition alive today on his innovative, independent label."

VAN MORRISON

"It was 20 years ago today, or thereabouts, when I first saw and heard Mick Hucknall sing. His voice and songs were as distinct then as they are now. One couldn't help but listen. He was a great songwriter and performer then and continues to grow every year on all levels. I can only wish him continued success.

I can still imagine Mick writing and performing many many years from now. He has a quality and strength about his work that will endure. Only time will tell... in fact it already has!"

JULIAN LENNON

"When I first heard 'Holding Back The Years' in 1985 it was such an event for me to see this young kid from Manchester with this sound. Gave me a thrill to hear a new voice on the horizon. I knew he was going to do great things. He has a way with a song because his voice has so much to say within it."

LAMONT DOZIER

"Simply Red are absolutely brill. Fairground is my fave."

FRANKIE DETTORI

"I put Mick Hucknall in the top five of great British pop singers. I first became aware of Simply Red when they did 'Money's Too Tight To Mention' and thought how good they were. Then when I heard Stars I thought it was so good I put it on the juke box in my house. It was just a great record.

We became friends and did the Audience With show together and ended up singing in the bar afterwards... doing soul tunes from Otis Redding and Solomon Burke, stuff we realised we both liked.

Mick has a way with songs and he has a unique sounding voice – you know it's him. That's the big difference between people who last and people who don't. You have to have your own style and Mick does. You always know it's him singing and he's fearless in terms of what he is prepared to sing. If he likes something he'll usually do it irrespective of what people think."

TOM JONES

"Mick Hucknall and Simply Red have created one of the greatest catalogues of songs over the past 20 years. Mick is the complete artist, both as a writer and a performer. His live shows are 'simply' the best I have ever seen! I look forward to the next chapter of Simply Red music."

DAVID COULTHARD

"Identical. The same voice, with the same sorrow, the same unmatched colour, the same inexorable talent bonded on every note. I was shocked. We were having a coffee break during a recording session in the studio. Who was singing like Billie Holiday? I turned around and there he was: Mick Hucknall. A very pleasant surprise. Pop music is not all his world. There is much more in his voice, of course, but especially in his head. Grande Mick!"

MINA

"From falling in love with the album Stars and the band Simply Red, my respect and admiration for Mick has steadily grown over the years. Being an R&B fan, I simply love how he so intelligently uses his fantastic vocal range (a subject of much envy) and interprets songs in such a sensitive and spirited way. He does it so effortlessly and beautifully. I am very proud to know him as a friend."

FRIDA LYNGSTAD

"I have been married to Kathryn for 20 years and we have been fans of Simply Red for all of them. Music, songs and a voice that has stood the test of time and that will fill our hearts forever. We both thank you for that."

STEVE MCLAREN

SOMETHING GOT ME STARTED

SOMETHING GOT ME STARTED

"I started singing when I was about three and I've been singing ever since."

So it goes that Elvis Presley began his singing career at the age of ten when he climbed on a chair to reach the microphone and sang his first version of 'Old Shep' to an audience of just a few hundred folks gathered at the Mississippi-Alabama Fair and Trade Dairy Show in Tupelo.

John Lennon was six years older when, inspired by Elvis, his career took off as his newly formed skiffle group The Quarry Men began playing at friends' parties and local talent contests around Liverpool.

Mick Hucknall beat them both when, at the tender age of five, he got up on stage at a family wedding in Manchester and, wearing Austrian lederhosen, gave a performance of 'I Want To Hold Your Hand', backed by the professional band booked as the reception entertainment.

What neither the red-haired kid from the Denton district of Manchester, nor the great British public knew was that this two-minute-plus rendition of The Beatles' fifth single and their third number one – co-written by Mick's new-found hero John Lennon and his songwriting pal Paul McCartney – was to be the start of something genuinely important in the annals of British pop music.

"I used to stand in front of the mirror holding a yardstick pretending to be John Lennon – I always wanted to be a singer."

It was also a moment which, over 40 years later, is still a treasured memory for both the mother of the bride and the woman who was being celebrated on her special day.

Nellie Spike and her family lived close to Mick and his dad Reg and, after Mick's mum left the marital home when he was just three years of age, she became the major female influence in his young life.

"I was ordinary in the sense that I was from a working class background but extraordinary in the sense that my father brought me up without my mother at all, which I imagine even now is very challenging for a man. In the 1960s that was unbelievable because nobody did it and everybody told him it couldn't be done but he's a very strong-willed person."

It was at Nellie's daughter Sheila's wedding that Mick gave what has gone on record as his first live concert. "The wedding reception was in the Festival Hall, Denton, and we hired a live band to play at the reception," recalls the bride. "Michael got up on stage wearing these lederhosen my sister Jennifer brought back for him from Austria and he just sang. He had bags of confidence and I think from then I knew he had the talent."

The lederhosen, it seems, wasn't the only outfit that Mick was given as a young child growing up in the north west of England. "He always wanted a Beatles suit," says Nellie who promptly set off to C&A and got him one... and that was not all she bought him. "I got him a little plastic guitar from Woolworths in Liverpool as well."

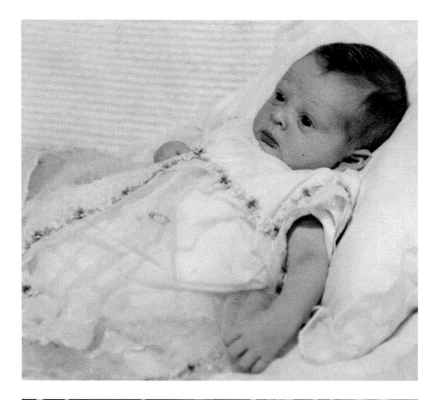

"I was introduced to music as a youngster by television – black-and-white television, everything seemed to be black-and-white when I was a kid, especially in Manchester. The family that sort of helped take care of me at that time – the Spike family – Sheila especially was very keen on 1960s music. She had a record player and used to play records quite a lot. It was really just The Beatles and I used to be able to find my favourite Beatles songs on the albums by the size of the grooves on the vinyl.

In the north west it was much bigger than just The Beatles being big, it was more than that. You are talking about a class culture that in the 1960s was unbelievable. You were expected to be married between the ages of 19 and 24 if you were a girl; if you weren't married by the time you were 24 you were weird, had something wrong with you, or couldn't have babies.

That was the sort of culture I was brought up into and The Beatles were the first people that represented us being able to get out of what we were in and showing that they could make it in the world.

It was pretty clear early on that they were much bigger than just Merseybeat. It was a whole north west thing. They were from Liverpool and that was good enough, they were close by. Before them it was Gracie Fields and George Formby, which was very different. The Beatles were a huge inspiration for the people in the north west – that you could actually get out of it."

So, armed with his Beatles suit and a plastic guitar, Mick became a regular turn at birthday parties and family get-togethers and was apparently never backward in coming forward. "He was full of it," is Nellie's description of the up-and-coming singer. "They loved him and he loved them wanting him to sing. He loved being the centre of attention but he didn't overdo it, he wasn't cheeky and was never a show-off."

Top: Mick at two weeks, June 1960   Bottom: Blithfield Hall, Staffs, August 1964

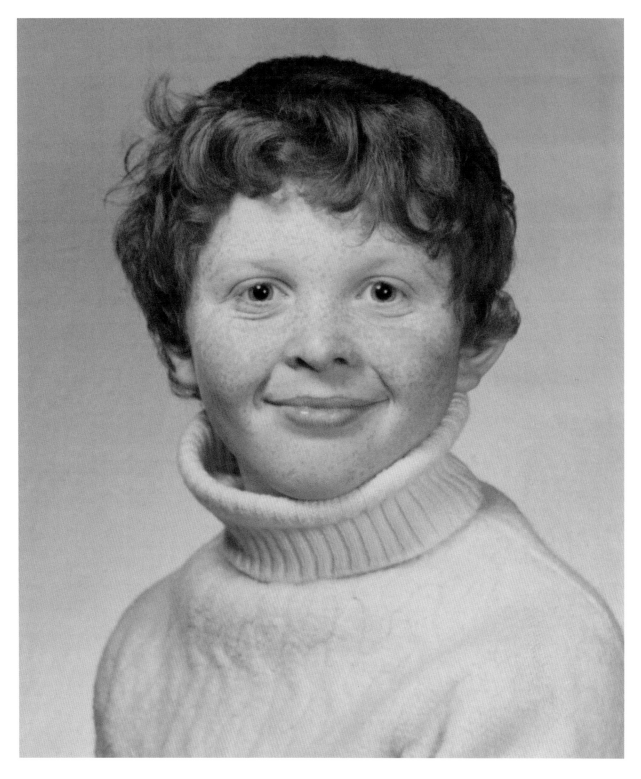

At St Lawrence's Primary School, Denton

Mick, aged eight, and his father Reg

Sadly one man who missed the wedding-day debut show was Mick's dad Reg, who was busy at his place of work in the centre of Manchester. "Being a barber, Saturday was always my busiest day so I missed out on a lot of family events and Sheila's wedding was one I didn't get to."

Even if he missed out on his son's live debut, Reg still played his part in Mick's musical education. From the days of sitting down together to listen to Radio Luxembourg broadcast the Top 20 on a Sunday night through to Terry Wogan's morning show on the BBC – coupled with visits to his dad's barber's shop, where the radio was a constant companion – music slowly but surely began to dominate Mick's life.

"Dad was always a music lover and right from a very early age we had discussions about what was going to be a hit record or not. We'd hear something on the radio, a new song by someone or other. When he was working, in his barber's shop, I think he had the radio on all day so he'd hear new songs on the radio. I wouldn't hear them as much but he'd say, 'Right listen to that, that's going to be a hit that, I'm telling you.' It was almost like horse racing, which is another one of his passions and I wouldn't be at all surprised if he had bets on them becoming hits. He had a good ear and still does."

Sheila Allott – as she now is – probably had the biggest influence on Mick, even though there was a 12 year age difference between them. She was already in her teens when her family began to help take care of Mick and, like every other teenager in the 1960s, she worshipped the groups that were making all the headlines. "I had posters of all the groups on my bedroom walls but mostly The Beatles, and I remember taking Michael to see *A Hard Day's Night* when he was about six or seven."

When Reg bought her family a record player for Christmas, Mick could then listen to Sheila's collection of 1960s hits including The Beatles, The Hollies and the Dave Clark Five, but one particular song sticks in her mind. "I remember him standing over the record player singing to the music and my most vivid memory is of him singing along to 'Michael Row The Boat Ashore'. Whenever I hear that song it reminds me of Michael."

"Motown was the first real attraction because I was buying pop singles from about 11 years old onwards. I knew of them before then but I didn't get my first record player until my 11th birthday. Then I started buying second-hand singles and then new releases with the money I'd get from doing milk rounds, paper rounds – I was always doing lots of jobs so I had money in my pocket. Every Saturday, I'd go shopping for records and started building up a collection of Motown and Stax and stuff like that – this was when I was between 11 and 13. But it was still mixed in with The Beatles, Led Zeppelin – their second album was a huge record for me – and the Stones. Their Sticky Fingers *was the first album I ever bought.*

I remember people remarking how ugly the Rolling Stones were, saying that they looked like ape men. I think that put a chord in my head for some time to

come – this perception of ugliness. The Stones were sort of neolithic but great because of that. It's actually something to do more with character than fulfilling an archetypal image of things. Surprising images can happen – Hendrix in a way was a surprising image."*

While Mick never got any real musical instruments as gifts from his father, his uncle arrived one day bearing an accordion for his young nephew, who was suitably unimpressed with the bizarre present. "He always said it was a stupid bloody present," recounts Reg. "He never played it and in the end flogged it in some second-hand shop."

Slowly Mick's musical tastes expanded from the Fab Four and even though Manchester was making its own impression on the pop music map with the likes of The Hollies, Freddie & The Dreamers, Wayne Fontana and Herman's Hermits, a young man's fancy ultimately turned towards soul music.

Liverpool was a Mecca for new music as returning seamen brought back the latest hits from America. As these records made their way into the Northern clubs, pubs and shops, so Mick became aware of soul stars such as The Supremes, Four Tops and Otis Redding, the earthy blues of Sonny Boy Williamson and John Lee Hooker and the man who became his biggest musical hero – James Brown, the Godfather of Soul. He satisfied this early obsession by using the money he scraped together from paper and milk rounds to buy records – old and new – from shops and market stalls.

"The Stones were influenced by blues and soul and that's how I've always seen my role two generations later. Some of my influences were from records these acts made of other old songs except that we had this wonderful opportunity at the beginning of the 1960s to see these black American artists for the first time, albeit you couldn't see them very well on some of the televisions we had at that time.

I remember those shiny suits the Four Tops used to wear and the glittering outfits of Diana Ross and The Supremes, and they'd come out at you from the TV. Music was a big part of my life right from early on – from three or four years old."

Growing up in Manchester in the early 1960s as an only child brought up by his father made Mick a strong, and some would say, boisterous youth who found life at Audenshaw Grammar School particularly hard to take. There was rugby instead of soccer, bullying teachers and, worst of all, most of his mates had failed the eleven-plus examination and gone to secondary modern schools.

"It's a big issue for me, the difference between grammar school and secondary school. The choice that I made – that was made for me – really had a big impact on who I am today, because that was the darkest time of my life. Between 11 and 16 was the most trying time ever in my life. I was in an alien school and it was not where I was from.

There was nothing there for me, but to be fair when I got to about 15 a guy came and played Pink Floyd albums, which was cool, but that was about it.

There was absolutely no creative outlet for anybody who had any artistic abilities. That's the big difference between being a pen-pusher or academically intelligent as opposed to being sensitively intelligent. I had no outlet so therefore you spend four years feeling useless because you don't think you are good at anything and a huge void was filled by getting drunk and rebelling against the entire institution."

But, in the midst of all this despair in his young life, Mick still had music and he was determined to enjoy it at every opportunity. The Northern Soul scene was at its height and while he drew the line at the all-dancing, pill-popping all-nighters, he did become a bit of a regular at the clubs, pubs and discos on the circuit.

"I was a little young to be really part of that Wigan scene. I was about 12 – just a bit under the radar to get into some of the places that did the all-nighters. I just used to go to ones in Manchester and we'd do all these sort of dance routines – twirling around and somersaults – I wouldn't do somersaults but I could do a flop on the floor, spins and all that kind of stuff. It was a great time, a lot of fun."

Alongside the music, Mick also developed a taste for beer during these regular visits to clubland and, aged 14, he satisfied this thirst by getting a job collecting glasses at the nearby Broomstair Working Men's Club to help finance his two passions. But not everybody was happy with this new arrangement. "I didn't like him working at that club," says Nellie. "He was too young and I didn't like the people there. They were rough and rude. I never went in there but you heard the stories."

However it was not all bad news from the Broomstair Club, according to Reg. "He used to make fairly good money with the tips and stuff and I think he probably picked up a bit from watching the turns they had on. Seeing them perform, he probably got to know how to use a microphone and use the stage."

While his basic school education was being enriched by nights spent in pubs and discos or working in a seedy club, Mick's dad had his own idea of a career for his son. "I tried to get him interested in fish farming and even suggested he went to Liverpool and study marine biology. I told him there was a great future in it and there would have been! But he just wasn't interested, I couldn't even get him to go fishing with me."

"The key moment is when you choose what you want to do. It's almost as if you take something for granted; that this is what I am going to do, but you don't know how you are going to go about doing it. So I believed that I was going to be a pop star from an early age – something like nine or ten years old. It was a fantasy. You live in a little bit of a Billy Liar world, a bit like every other kid who daydreams and has this kind of fantasy.

I respect my father deeply for everything he did for me but he had absolutely no influence on my career at all. He wouldn't accept that I might have a career in music but he just had to live with it. But I had a complete and utter faith that's what I was going to do, much to my father's disapproval and him wanting me to be

Top: Mick aged thirteen (centre) at Audenshaw Grammar School

Right: Whitechapel Street, London, 1983

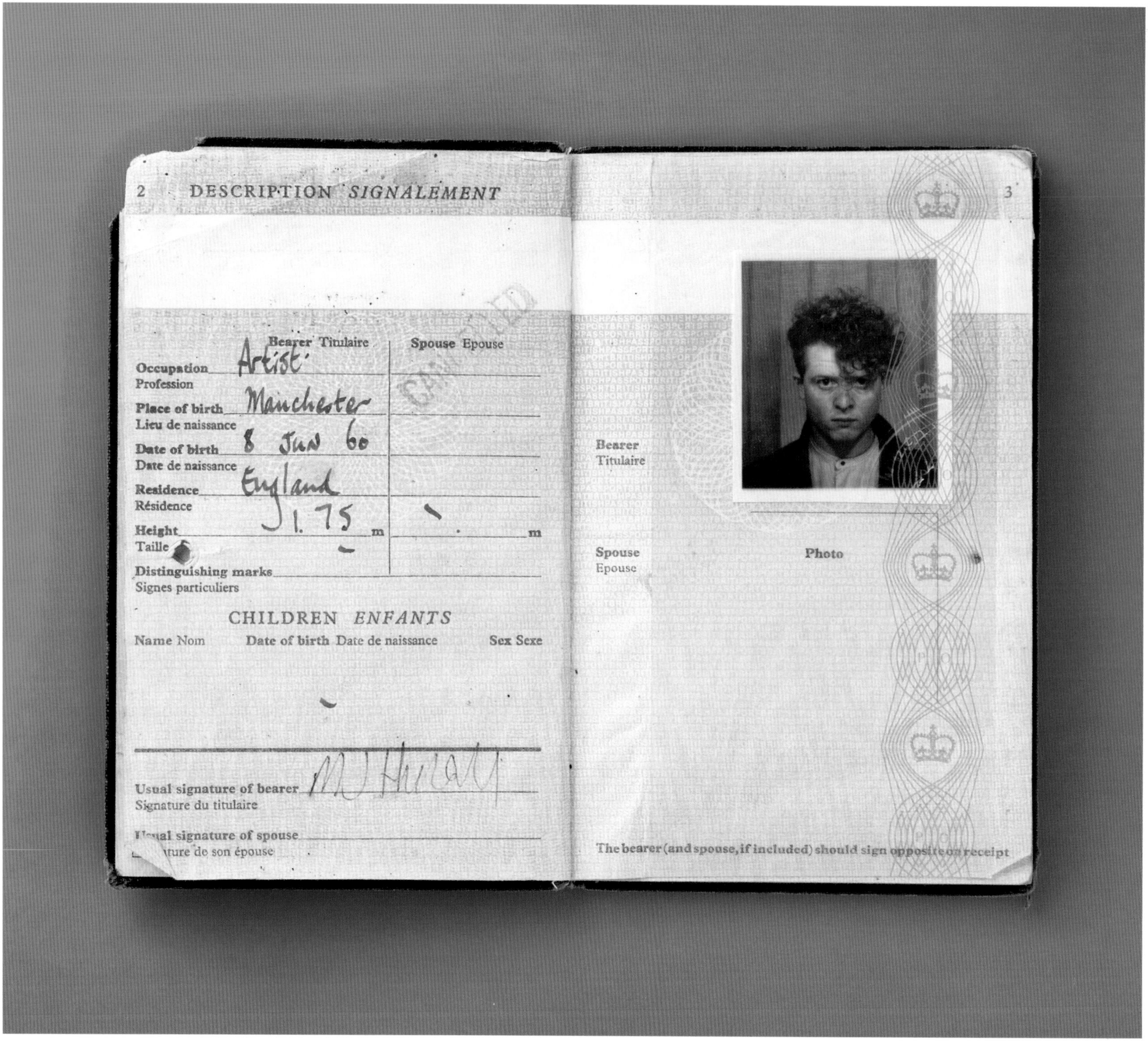

	Bearer Titulaire	Spouse Epouse
Occupation Profession	Artist	
Place of birth Lieu de naissance	Manchester	
Date of birth Date de naissance	8 Jun 60	
Residence Résidence	England	
Height Taille	1.75 m	m
Distinguishing marks Signes particuliers		

CHILDREN *ENFANTS*

Name Nom	Date of birth Date de naissance	Sex Sexe

Usual signature of bearer Signature du titulaire

Usual signature of spouse Signature de son épouse

Bearer Titulaire

Spouse Epouse   Photo

The bearer (and spouse, if included) should sign opposite on receipt *a marine biologist. Oddly I do have a great interest in marine life now and love the water and see that now it could have been a great career."*

Finally in 1976, with three O' level passes to his credit, Mick left the grammar school he hated so much and moved on to Tameside College of Further Education and a two-year art course. And everybody was quick to notice a difference.

"I thought he'd settle down eventually (at grammar school) but going to the Sixth Form College was a good thing, it was a different environment completely," says his father, while Nellie, who was gradually losing touch with the growing teenager, saw a change too. "At the college he became a bit of an exhibitionist and a bit of rebel but he was clever. He got a degree, but he did it his way."

His way involved a new look and, without much money to finance his lifestyle, Mick took to the charity shops and market stalls around Manchester. He collected, among other things, a maxi-length raincoat, a 50p hacking jacket and even a British Rail jacket, and together they brought him a certain new standing in the community. "He did get a reputation of being a bit of a weirdo because of the way he dressed," recalls Reg, "but I think he quite liked people staring at him."

As the clothes became more outrageous, Reg decided to concentrate on his son's hair. For him the 1960s and The Beatles had been a nightmare as the fashion for long hair gripped the nation. People still had haircuts but fewer of them and they no longer wanted a traditional short-back-and-sides. All this took its toll on the number of barber's shops needed to deal with the demands of modern day grooming.

"I always tried to give him a good haircut and I've cut it in all sorts of fashions but there was a period when I just refused to cut it and said, 'Well if you want to go round looking like an idiot that's your business.'"

Idiot or not, Mick stuck to his guns, worked his way through college and went on to Manchester Polytechnic and a three-year degree course in Fine Art, where he was able to indulge his love of music and fashion to his heart's content.

"I started writing songs when I was about 15. I tried to write with a band before the Frantic Elevators and managed to write one song, but then I met Neil Moss and we started writing songs together. He hated the name Moss and thought it was cool to have another name so he chose Smith.

He and his brother Ian had a great passion for music and so did I, and we just kind of exchanged ideas. Their parents were fantastically understanding, they had a record player in the living room and they let Ian play Who records at about volume number 9 while they sat there.

The first ideas for songwriting came directly from Ian coming back having seen the Pistols and describing what had happened. We were all at a bit of a loss; you had like David Bowie and some people doing some progressive work but it was all getting a bit – 30 minute guitar solos, concept albums, three tracks on an entire

piece of vinyl, 17 minute blues pieces, people turning their backs on the audience when they played, Persian carpets, groupies on the side. It all started to get a bit too regal and it didn't relate to a spotty 15-year-old from Manchester."

While his dad was filling the house with the sounds of Matt Monro, Nat King Cole and The Three Degrees, Mick, in the mid-1970s, was busy latching onto a whole new movement that brought not only a different kind of music but also represented the attitude of a new generation.

Punk and the Sex Pistols arrived in Manchester during the summer of 1976 and hearing their music and revelling in their anarchic message was enough to convince Mick that here was a route he could follow.

"Punk was great. It was rebelling against everything, including music. It woke you up to the fact that a lot of energy and excitement had been taken out of music.

You think about the story of Quadrophenia, *The Who album. It's a very punk concept and in a way it told the story before the story had actually happened. That whole cut-your-hair-off thing – I did that on Walney Beach near Barrow-in-Furness. Out in this National Park on my bike and I cut my hair off on the beach. It fitted in, so key to the exact right time in my generation – 16 years old, John Lydon and especially the Buzzcocks.*

They had an interesting line-up with Howard Devoto and a great tension. You had this sort of pop thing that Pete Shelley had but then Devoto had this art thing as well and it was just a great combination. It was a shame it was so short. They were really the ones that got me and Neil excited. Neil went to see the Sex Pistols Anarchy tour at the Electric Circus and that's when we decided to put the band together. We'd started writing songs in the late summer of 1976."

"The first time I ever saw him on the telly was at a punk show with Siouxsie and the Banshees and he was right at the front of the crowd," recalls his Dad. "But I couldn't take punk seriously. I mean I quite liked some of it – The Buzzcocks and Sham 69 and that send up of 'My Way' by Sid Vicious – but I didn't see any future in it; it wasn't going to last."

Mick's debut on TV had in fact been a punk showcase at Belle Vue which Granada filmed – capturing Mick in mid-pogo – and shown regularly over the next few years. At the same time, The Buzzcocks and Joy Division were among the first local bands to emerge and make a name for themselves; a situation that ignited the first flames of ambition in Mick's belly.

"We were not doing performances at that time but Neil and I were going to all these punk gigs. I saw everybody else apart from the Pistols; the Ramones, the first Motorhead gig in Manchester. They were amazing – I know they were heavy metal but Lemmy is a star, I love Lemmy – the Television/Blondie tour, The Clash. I saw so many great acts.

I saw The Fall about 15 to 20 times and we actually toured with The Fall, we did a whole tour of the north east of England – Leeds and Scarborough –

supporting *The Fall. Our second gig was with Sham 69, we supported Magazine, so we did a lot of stuff. They were early days and usually there were only about 50 to 100 people in the place."*

Mick started the Frantic Elevators sometime in late 1977 with a ramshackle and fluid line-up which included Brian Turner, his drinking pal from the days of the Broomstair Club, childhood friend Neil Moss (a.k.a Neil Smith), Steve Tansley and Mark Reeder. A year later there was a more stable line-up featuring Mick, Moss, Turner and Kevin Williams.

If their roots were in punk, they failed to convince Mick's dad. "Although they were punk he didn't have all the weird hair and safety pins but it was a grounding for him I suppose."

As the Elevators rehearsed and gigged around the north of England, Mick slowly but surely developed a taste for life in a band and, more importantly, a career in music, although Reg was still to be convinced. "In those early days I was never really convinced that he was going to make a career out of it. In fact at one point when he was in the Frantic Elevators, I very nearly talked him out of the idea. I always told him that the music business was a dirty bitchy business and I was right. I said it's hard to make it to the top."

"Me, Neil, Kev and Brian were the long-standing band but early on there were other members who came from closer, in the Denton area. Once we started doing gigs and going to all these shows we made a lot of connections and started to get offers of doing more gigs ourselves. So Kevin came from Oldham and Brian came from the Droylsden area; we weren't actually that close but Manchester put us together.

The Fall, I think it's safe to say, was our only tour. That was when we'd made it in the business, we did like four gigs in a row. I'll never forget one night we had to sleep in the back of a transit van we were renting from Salford Van Hire. Instead of going back to Manchester we decided that we'd drive to Scarborough and then just do the gig the next day. So we parked on the sea-front and slept in this van with the wind blowing outside. We got up at about 6.30 in the morning, full of beer and hangovers and these huge waves just smashed into us. And we did the gig in Scarborough that night. That was rock 'n' roll!"

Around this time Manchester was becoming home to an important and influential new record label where the hits and headlines were matched by feelings of admiration, dismay and even mistrust. Factory Records gave life to the likes of Joy Division, Happy Mondays and New Order and also gave birth to the city's notorious Hacienda Club.

But it was an aspect of Manchester that Mick and his mates were not interested in pursuing, and the Elevators continued to carve out an existence touring around the north of England while dreaming of success on an altogether bigger scale.

Top: Nellie and Alf Spike (centre)   Bottom: Mick and Nellie
with their daughters

Frantic Elevators

FRANTIC ELEVATORS

Holding Back The Years

Holding Back The Years

Holding Back The Years

NO WAITING

————————FRANTIC ELEVATORS————————

A SIDE **Holding back the years.~Pistols in my brain.** 1 SIDE

SONGS WRITTEN, ARRANGED AND PRODUCED BY HUCKNALL & MOSS

MICK HUCKNALL — GUITAR · VOCALS

NIEL SMITH — GUITAR · VOCALS · PIANO

BRIAN TURNER — BASS GUITAR · PIANO

KEVIN WILLIAMS — DRUMS · PERCUSSION

Frantic's H.Q. 061 - 226-2728

Recorded at Hologram, Stockport, engineered by Tim. Photos and artwork by Watty. Many thanks to Roger Eagle, Elliot Rashman, Steve Mardi, Richard Watt and Steve Smethurst.

This is a **production** AUGUST 1982

COUSINS 985 4211

"I was the complete antithesis of everything Factory, the Hacienda and what the Manchester movement stood for... and still am. I respect what they've done but it's not how I would have gone about doing it. It was not what I wanted to do. They were culture with a small c and art with a capital A. For me it's the other way round. I write to communicate with as many people as possible. I like the idea that people share my emotions on a million-scale basis. I love that. It's the biggest prize.

It was very much a Manchester clique and we were never part of it because we were quite happy people. They had groups pretending to be unhappy or in some cases people who were very unhappy and I always found the aura around that whole scene quite dark and a bit austere and, dare I say it, anal.

Just seeing Factory as it initially was – this kind of black-and-white, I've-been-to-Berlin poster, all black, black makeup, everyone walking around the Hacienda oh-so-serious – that was what it was like in the beginning. There are a lot of myths about that place, it was empty most of the time and it was only Ecstasy and the Happy Mondays that kicked it off. But to be fair, New Order and Joy Division have done some great work – no doubt about that and it's lasted the test of time. I'd never criticise that, I think that's really great. But we were completely alien, we were from entirely different worlds."

One of the band's early gigs brought Mick back into contact with the girl who had introduced him to music over ten years earlier. Sheila, whose wedding Mick had sung at, had lost contact when Mick went off to college but they were reunited one Saturday morning in Manchester. "He must have been about 18 or 19 when he suddenly appeared in the Kenning Car Hire offices where I was working. He was with the rest of the group and they wanted to hire a transit for the night. I think they had a gig in Yorkshire that night."

If Sheila had lost contact, Nellie was still in the picture and keen to know what her "adopted" son was up to. "I never saw his group but he brought me the first record they made and signed it for me. He always told me where they were playing and what they were doing and I thought that things were picking up for them, but there was a lot of travelling and lots of ups-and-downs."

As a result of their live work, the Frantic Elevators built up a bit of a following and something of a reputation and this, in turn, led them towards their first record deal and the release of their debut single in 1979. The songs 'Voices In The Dark', 'Passion' and 'Every Day I Die' came out on the local TJM label and were followed a year later by 'You Know What You Told Me' on Eric's Records. In 1981 they issued their third single in three years with 'Searching For The Only One' on Crackin' Up.

Needless to say, success did not automatically follow in the footsteps of these releases but the second single brought Mick together with Roger Eagle who ran Eric's club in Liverpool – a regular haunt for Mick and the band who rehearsed in the city – and the label of the same name. He and his partner Pete Fulwell took over management of the Frantic Elevators, issued a single and actually recorded a live album of R&B music which remains unreleased to this day.

But more importantly Eagle began to introduce the musically hungry Mick to a whole menu of new sounds and styles which were to stay with him and influence him throughout his musical career.

"The transition in music isn't as remarkable or as bizarre as some people would have you think. When you look at a lot of the artists – the new punk stuff, the first four releases from Stiff Records, the first Elvis Costello album, Ian Dury & the Blockheads, the first two Rolling Stones albums I had, and you hear the Velvet Underground and Iggy Pop and some 1960s kind of garage stuff – it all suddenly starts to sound like the same thing.

Me and Neil used to be listening to this kind of stuff. 'Honest I Do' was the first time I heard about Jimmy Reed and then I went out and bought the Carnegie Hall *album and played the death out of it around the same time as everybody was listening to 'Anarchy In The UK'... and so was I.*

Later on, another person who was very instrumental was Roger Eagle. He played a very important part in my musical understanding and influences because he brought dub reggae onto my menu with King Tubby and Lee Scratch Perry plus more obscure R&B and jazz from Charlie Mingus, John Coltrane and Miles Davis and that was just like me being in a library full of candy-flavoured music. He was a musical teacher to me, a bit of a guru but he didn't really go past the 1970s."

Around the time of the release of 'You Know What You Told Me', music journalist Johnny Waller caught up with the Frantic Elevators in Liverpool and produced the first major feature on the band in *Sounds*.

He wrote: "Vocalist Mick, a bundle of nervous enthusiasm in a ludicrously bright Bermuda shirt, greets me cheerily," and went on to describe his meeting with the band's "token nutter" Brian Turner. "An all-purpose lunatic and rumoured to be the band's bassist (when I first met him two years ago he told me he was sure to be kicked out since he could never play in time... whatever, he's still there)."

He described the band's first single 'Voice In the Dark' as "a three-song delight that pulled in different directions leaving me unsure of the future for them," and quoted Mick as saying, "I'd like hit singles, yeah, and I think anybody who doesn't must be an idiot, must be a clown. It would be very nice to have a hit."

That said, Waller ended up with an encouraging critique of the follow-up single 'You Know What You Told Me'. "Any initial doubts are soon dismissed by its naïve off-beat waltz appeal and the tenderness of the lyrics. It's as infectious as hell and deserves to be a hit (but won't be)."

It wasn't, and gradually it dawned on the band that they had no real future in a world of punk music. Mick was certainly hankering after a different style of music and the band's last single was a genuine sign of things to come.

'Holding Back The Years' was probably the second song Mick ever wrote and Reg remembers Mick and fellow band member and credited co-composer Moss

highlife Holidays

Mediterranean Apartment Holidays (International) Limited
20 Cotton Lane, Manchester, M20 9UX
Telephone: 061-434 8331
Telex: 665421 onward

NAME: MICHAEL JAMES HUCKNALL
BORN: 1960, DENTON, MANCHESTER. ONLY CHILD, PARENTS DIVORCED
BROUGHT UP BY FATHER + FRIENDS.
SCHOOLING: St LAWRENCES PRIMARY, AUDENSHAW GRAMMAR SCHOOL, TAMESIDE
COLLEGE of FURTHER EDUCATION, MANCHESTER POLYTECHNIC SCHOOL of FINE ART
POSSESSES BA (HONS) DEGREE in FINE ART.

OBSESSIONS; MUSIC, PAINTING, COOKING, CLYNES WINE BAR (for its guinness doesn't
sell wine!) WOMEN, POOL + SNOOKER, CYCLING + SWIMMING.

MUSIC. SANG in FIRST BAND AT 15 played pubs + clubs, formed FRANTIC
ELEVATORS in JULY 1977. first gig with them JAN 1978. MADE FOUR
RECORDS.' VOICE in the DARK (TJM) YOU KNOW WHAT YOU TOLD ME (ERICS)
        SEARCHING FOR the only ONE (CRACKIN' UP) HOLDING BACK the YEARS (No waiting)
After 'You know what you told me' was managed briefly by Pete Fulwell then
worked closely with Roger Eagle 'my greatest mentor', worked as
DJ for him and discovered great influential music through him.
Left the Elevators in NOV '82 now he's all alone (aw!)
        MUSICAL INFLUENCES

Arthur Alexander, Bobby Bland, James Brown, Tim Buckley, Ray Charles,
Steve Cropper, JB's guitar player, (who is he?) Bo Diddley, John Coltraine,
L+P. Chess, Al Jackson, John Lennon, Charlie Mingus, George
Martin, Lee Perry, Charlie Parker, Otis Redding, Little Richard,
Mc Cartney's bass playing, Keith Richard, Jimi Hendrix, King Tubby, Spector,
Charlie Watts, Ringo Starr, Stevie Wonder, Howlin' Wolf, Muddy Waters,
Little Walter, Sonny Boy Williamson 1 + 2, Big Youth, Burning Spear. etc...

Registered in England No. 158650 at 106 Barlowmoor Road, Manchester M20 8PN.

working on the track in his house. "Neil had a guitar and they'd go upstairs and practice all the time. I was sick of hearing 'Holding Back The Years' – they played it so often I used to shout up at them to turn it down."

"I wrote 'Holding Back The Years' in its entirety. The reason I gave Neil a credit was because of the time we spent together, because of those years when we'd not had any success. In the beginning we did write some songs together but after a while we started to have our own ideas and then have these meetings on a Friday night in my bedroom when we'd play out the songs and work them out together. We just came to an agreement that we'd call it Hucknall/Moss and that was it..."

Written in 1977, the song finally came out in 1982 on the No Waiting label with a sleeve featuring Mick in a striped tank top with a revolver in his mouth. The tasteless photo was linked to the B-side 'Pistols In My Brain' and had overtones of an earlier Eddie & The Hot Rods record cover for 'Woolly Bully'. Whether it was because of the cover or the songs we'll never know, but either way the record failed to make an impression despite Mick resorting to putting it on the jukeboxes in local pubs and clubs.

Now resident in his own flat, Mick was combining playing with the Elevators with finishing his studies at the Poly when a new opportunity came along. He took to the turntables and began to make a name for himself as a local DJ, which made him even more determined to find a way into the music business. By now, even Reg had come to accept the inevitable. "When he got his degree I thought that at least he could always get a job teaching so decided to leave it in the lap of the gods and let him go for it."

In fact, Mick didn't go for it for too much longer, at least not with the Frantic Elevators. In 1983 he announced he was leaving the band as his aspirations turned towards finding a more soulful outlet for his musical ambitions.

"After we'd been going with the Elevators for quite a number of years I started thinking that I needed to get this thing moving. I was living in this place in Hulme, in this flat which was quite nice inside but in a difficult area and after about four years I needed to get out of there and start making things happen."

This new determination would take Mick through three different line-ups under four different names before finally bringing him into contact with the first of the two men who would change his life and steer him towards stardom within two short years.

"It was around that time that I met Elliot Rashman, who was working at Manchester Polytechnic. I'd met him before, he was a friend of a friend and he wanted to manage me. Initially he offered to manage the Frantic Elevators but it didn't take long to realise that he wanted to get me out of there and put another band around me. He wasn't devious at all, he was quite open about it."

Mick's handwritten 'CV'

World Service line-up (Mick right) formed
between Frantic Elevators and Simply Red,
Manchester 1983

FAIRGROUND

FAIRGROUND

"Through years of experience you hone a way to communicate your music to an audience."

Since October 1984, when Simply Red, born and bred in the heart of Lancashire, first took to the stage in, of all places, Yorkshire, they have gone on to play over 800 concerts across every continent and in very nearly every country around the world.

From the humble beginnings of Northern clubs with crowds of just a couple of hundred to an audience of over 80,000 in one of the world's most famous soccer stadia, Simply Red have taken their music to the world and the world has listened.

The promoter of one of the band's earliest gigs was Manchester-based PR man Andy Spinoza who, back then, was a leading light in the magazine *City Life* and he remembers it wasn't a particularly profitable night for the fledgling publication.

"It was the gig at which Simply Red got signed but we didn't actually make any money because Elliot had about 80 people on the guest list who got in free, and that was our margin between a profit and a loss."

"I think of the first few gigs we did, two were at Manchester Poly and one of them was supporting Alexei Sayle, but he wouldn't know that. There were about 400 people at that one and we were called something like the Dancing Dead because we were still searching for a name. We'd done one before with about 200 people and then at the next gig there were about 1,500."

Journalist Adrian Thrills, currently rock critic with the *Daily Mail*, was working on *NME* when he first saw the band in early 1985 during their first trip south to London. "I went to see them do a gig at London University which wasn't even in the main hall – it was in the canteen, and there were no more than 120 people."

FROM MANCHESTER

SIMPLY RED

PLUS SUPPORT & DISCO

ONLY £2.00 ON DOOR 8 TILL LATE

FRIDAY MAY 17th. 1985

UNION HALL. GOLDSMITHS' COLLEGE, NEW CROSS. SE 14 6NW. TEL' 01 692 1406

But he still treasures that moment when he saw Mick and Simply Red for the first time. "You can't beat the first time you see a band, there's always something special about seeing a band before they're stars, when you're in on the secret," is his recollection of the night. "That gig in a canteen, hearing that voice for the first time, and thinking this band have really got something. And they came through in a boom time for British music."

Later in the year, the band made it on to the stage to support Mick's greatest musical hero James Brown and there, on those nights at the Hammersmith Odeon, working as an assistant producer on a music programme, was a woman who would later be involved in creating some of the most memorable images of Mick and Simply Red.

"We were doing the story of James Brown," says Zanna, "and it was a strange event because we had to take £25,000 in cash to pay him in order to do the film: it was all a bit scary." While she didn't take much notice of the support band, she does recall that they caught the producer's eye. "I remember him saying that they were a very interesting band."

"We did a show at Hammersmith Odeon with James Brown very early on in our career. Eric Clapton came to it and then invited us to join him on a home town gig in Guildford, which was fantastic.

We weren't allowed to speak to James Brown, the promoter told us to stay away. I remember on the first night he was watching us from the side of the stage wearing rollers and a hairnet. I was singing and there's James Brown in rollers and a hairnet – quite a sight!"

One man who first saw Simply Red a month earlier and is still working with the band to this day is Stuart Galbraith, the current Managing Director of Live Nation Music UK. In those days he was with promoters MCP and has promoted the band's UK shows since 1985 and their June 15 gig at Manchester International. "I remember it because it was my birthday," says Galbraith, who has booked everything from club shows to theatres, to arenas, stadiums and stately homes and, for the past six years, has also booked their international dates.

Since supporting Brown and an earlier tour with UB40, Simply Red have never appeared as a support act in the UK and Galbraith puts that down to a couple of things. "Right from the early days it was obvious that Mick was writing great songs that were radio-friendly and had great crossover appeal but they could also cut it live which, for a band of that genre at that time, was perhaps unusual."

From their first club tours, Simply Red quickly moved into theatre venues in support of the *Picture Book* album but, even at that early stage, Galbraith sensed that the pressure occasionally got to Mick. "There have been some traumatic periods and they probably go back as far as the first single because it all happened so quickly.

"We were touring an awful lot, and although I only got to see him on the road you could see he was struggling to deal with the sudden invasion of his privacy and the sudden projection of him becoming a star in the UK. In those early years, we certainly had a few superstar moments."

During 1985 Simply Red grew from venues such as The Pit at Leicester University and Goldsmith's College, London to the Civic Centre, Guildford – with Eric Clapton – and onto Brighton Conference Centre, the Free Trade Hall, Manchester and finally Wembley Arena.

Although they played the annual international Midem music business conference in Cannes in early 1985, it was their follow-up appearance in 1986 that brought them to the attention of their new UK record company East West, a division of WEA UK.

Warner Music International manager Anne-Marie Nicol had seen the band at Ronnie Scott's the previous year and been impressed so, when the time came for them to appear at the WEA International conference being held in Cannes during Midem, she sensed a new opportunity. "That show was a turning point as far as getting support from the upper echelons of the company. I'd been beetling away with label managers around the world but when you get a bunch of MDs in one room it can make a big difference. People went back to their companies and began to talk about Simply Red."

For the band's co-manager Andy Dodd this performance was also an axial moment in the story of Simply Red when, as he puts it, "fate inexorably intervened to our ultimate advantage." As the new boys performing at their record company's party in front of the legendary co-founder of Atlantic Records Neshui Ertegun, Mick and the band knew they faced a tough test and, as Dodd recalls, they came through with flying colours.

"Mick's performance was sensational and immediately after the show Neshui unexpectedly took to the stage and announced to the collected Warner executives that Mick had the best male voice he had heard in 25 years and that it was their job to go away from Midem and break the band on a worldwide basis.

"It was like God saying 'let there be light'," adds Dodd who remembers he and management partner Rashman looking at each other dumbstruck. "The rest, as they say, is history."

With the first album out it was essential that the touring continued in order to spread the word, and Nicol had her first taste of taking Simply Red onto the international stage, Italy and Germany responded with major sales of both records and tour dates. "They were doing all manner of shows around Europe, particularly in Italy, and you could see instantly that Mick took to the Italian

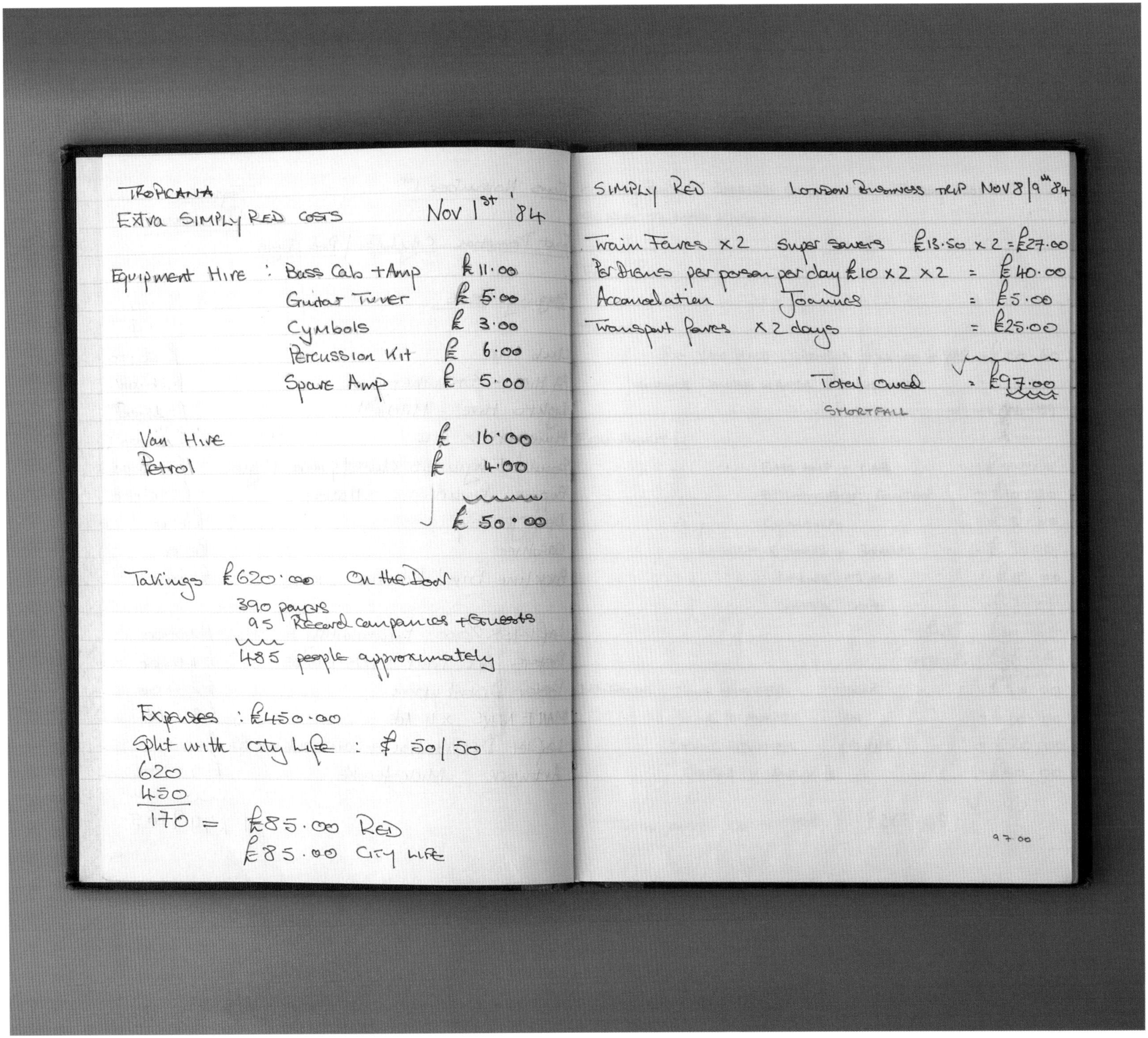

TROPICANA
EXtra SIMPLY RED COSTS   Nov 1st '84

Equipment Hire : Bass Cab + Amp   £ 11·00
                 Guitar Tuner   £ 5·00
                 Cymbols   £ 3·00
                 Percussion Kit   £ 6·00
                 Spare Amp   £ 5·00

Van Hire   £ 16·00
Petrol   £ 4·00
                                     ~~~~~~~
                                   √ £ 50·00

Takings £620·000   On the Door
         390 payers
          95 Record companies + Guests
         ~~~
         485 people approximately

Expenses : £450·00
Split with City Life : £ 50/50
620
450
___
170 = £ 85·00 RED
       £ 85·00 CITY LIFE

SIMPLY RED   LONDON Business TRIP NOV 8/9th '84

Train Fares x2   Super savers   £13·50 x 2 = £27·00
Per diems per person per day £10 x 2 x 2 = £40·00
Accomodation   Joannes   = £5·00
Transport fares   x 2 days   = £25·00

                        Total Owed   = £97·00
                         SHORTFALL

                                          97 00

Early tour accounts, November 1984

31

record company and to Italy as a country. We spent a lot of time there and he was selling out big shows in Italy."

Stefano Senardi was Head of International at Warner Music Italy, and his first experience of Simply Red live was when he accidentally caught them playing in a restaurant at somebody's private birthday party. Later that year he saw the real thing. "At the concert in San Siro football stadium in Milan they opened for Simple Minds but had the biggest success themselves, they were bigger than the bands they were supposed to support."

Watching them on the road, Nicol sensed that while Mick was getting better with every show, some of the band were not progressing at the same rate. "My feeling was that he wanted them to get better along with him, but some of the band seemed uncomfortable with their role and couldn't always be bothered."

While he didn't play on the *Picture Book* album or the UK leg of the tour, sax player Ian Kirkham was recruited in January 1986, in time for the European dates. "At the start it's all new and exciting but after a while you do feel like you are just going round again. But there's always something happening, there's new music to play and usually you get to go somewhere you haven't been before. It's a great life but you just have time to get back into a normal routine after one tour and you're off on the road again."

Never one to miss an opportunity, Mick used touring to work on new numbers that hadn't been recorded and the international dates promoting *Picture Book* saw two new songs appear in the show. "On that leg of the tour we began working on 'Infidelity' and 'Let Me Have It All'," says long-time band member Ian Kirkham. "We put 'Infidelity' together on the tour and then by the time we got back into the studio there were some other new songs we hadn't heard before, which Mick had presumably worked out on the road."

The *Picture Book* tour ran almost uninterrupted from October 1985 through to December 1986 and covered the UK, Europe and North America (twice) before ending up back in the UK for the run-up to Christmas. In that 15-month period they did shows in every month except March and October.

Spinoza was among those who kept going back for more and he remained impressed by what he heard. "The voice was sensational and when you went to shows with friends who were a bit dismissive of his records, they'd have to hold their hands up and admit it was a phenomenal live sound. There was a real up-beat quality about those gigs and they were probably some of the best I've sever seen."

Simply Red made their US debut during the *Picture Book* tour period and Kirkham has fond memories of the half-a-dozen shows that introduced the

San Siro Stadium with Simple Minds
and The Waterboys, Milan, July 1986

RIVIERA LIGURE
Tipica figura di pescatore
Typique figure de pêcheur
Typical figure of fisherman
Typischer Fischer

Ediz. Casa delle Cartoline - Sanremo - Tel. 0184-83729
300-044 da fotocolor

HA Hee Ho so I am
is a town where
everybody is typical
like this!?. Am I a
typical singer? Are
you typical people?
I'm having a good
Relaxing time

The Rest of US
SO WHAT LIMITED 1st floor
48 Princess ST
MANCHESTER
ENGLAND.

affectionately
Mickey Rosso x

band to the great American public. "It was the first time I'd ever been to the States. We started out in Canada and went on to America and played all these fabulous clubs like El Mocambo in Toronto, The Ritz in New York and the Palace in Hollywood."

From her position as press officer at Elektra, Lisa Barbaris relished having Mick and his band for a major 30-plus date tour of America but remembers it as something of a one-off experience. "He did a proper tour on the first album and it helped take *Picture Book* into the top 20, but he hasn't done another one since. In the last ten years I'd say Mick has spent less than 30 days in America."

However, she still believes that playing America could be the key to renewed success Stateside for Simply Red because they were heralded when they appeared in major cities such as New York, Chicago, San Francisco, Washington and Los Angeles, and his show at the Ritz in April 1986 remains a highlight to this day for Barbaris. "Shows like that still rank among people's top ten shows of all time. When they lost the power and he sang a cappella, it was musically one of the best moments I ever saw. That night he picked us up and took us to another place."

In the opening month of 1987, a new face joined the Simply Red touring team with the arrrival of Nick Levitt as stage manager. He was interviewed and hired on the same night as he saw them perform at Newcastle City Hall in the last month of 1986.

It was a time when the band were breaking out of the university and club circuit to go into larger halls and theatres, and this was followed very quickly by the move into arenas. Levitt joined a touring outfit that consisted of "a couple of trucks of equipment, simple lighting, a few risers and a backdrop – all fairly straightforward."

"The smaller venues are more intimate and in some ways you think you have to be more accurate with the way you sing but in actual fact you don't. You've got to be just as good and hit the notes just as well in a big venue as a small one. A lot of the time I've got my eyes shut anyway so I'm just getting on with singing the song."

Getting settled into the set-up was not easy for Levitt, who was very much the new kid on the block and someone who was looking to make changes. "It was tough at the start because the band had grown up with the crew but now things were getting more professional. It was a transitional period but bit by bit, over a couple of years, we changed personnel until we got who we thought should be the key people – and some of them are still with the band today."

Above all, Levitt appreciates the freedom he is given by the leader of the band. "He's trusting and loyal and has trusted me to bring in the team that makes it work on the road. We have a close professional relationship and he's very good

MCP *presents*

SIMPLY RED

MEN AND WOMEN TOUR

Plus Special Guests

BRIGHTON CENTRE
TUESDAY 17th APRIL
7.30 pm
Tickets: £7.00, £6.00
Available from B/O Tel: 0273 202881
and usual agents.

Filming 'Let Me Take You Home' video, 1990

Stage designs for *Life* Tour, 1995

at spotting very quickly who is professional and who's not. He doesn't tolerate fools and, even though he doesn't know every person's specific role, he gets a feel for who's doing what and who can be trusted."

As the new *Men And Women* album was released in early 1987 so Simply Red got back on the merry-go-round and went off on a tour that began in March and ran through pretty much uninterrupted until December that year, taking in over 120 shows.

New countries such as Japan, New Zealand and Australia were included in the schedule and Warner Music's Peter Ikin was among those who welcomed Simply Red when they arrived Down Under. "Their first tour was a pretty standard itinerary playing the best venues in the major cities including the 12,000-seater Sydney Entertainment Centre."

Because of the long distance involved in travelling to Australia, Simply Red couldn't make short promo trips for TV shows or radio spots, so Ikin and his team had to get the best out of them while they had them. "They did great shows, got great reviews, did loads of promotion and we sold heaps more records – so everyone was happy."

One person who accidentally benefited from Mick's debut visit to Japan was the clothes designer Paul Smith, who had been hired to produce the outfits for the tour. Anne-Marie Nicol watched two careers take off at the same time. "Smith was completely unknown in Japan as a designer but when Japanese television did a documentary about Simply Red, and mentioned their clothing, that launched him there as well."

This was the same Paul Smith who Mick had visited on the arm of then WEA executive Moira Bellas in 1985. "Moira took him along to get his first suit and I remember he raged for ages about the price of it at £400," recalls co-manager Andy Dodd.

As a regular member of the team that has steered Simply Red's live work, Galbraith is charged with coming up with venues and tours that, in addition to offering support to an album release, also make financial sense – and it's usually been a case of leaving 'em wanting more.

"It was a risk but the beauty with Simply Red is that we always underplayed the market so that on every single tour we did, we turned away business. The theory was that the people who couldn't get tickets for this tour would be the first people to buy tickets for the next dates."

His advice on tours and venues is important as Mick likes to see drawings of the venues with seating plans before moving onto the business part of the project. And it isn't just Mick who is in at the planning stage.

"In the early days, Andy Dodd and Elliot Rashman were a great team alongside Mick," recalls Galbraith. "Andy focused on the business side of it all while Elliot was there with Mick discussing the music and artistic aspects. Elliot was in some ways Mick's rottweiller; he was so passionate and determined and always looking to get the best out of any situation so that it benefited Mick."

After underplaying the *Men And Women* tour, Simply Red adopted the same principle for the tour in support of the 1989 album *A New Flame* – and with good reason, according to Galbraith. "We'd all heard the album and we knew the band was strong enough to go into arenas – it wasn't a big risk, it was just part of the band's natural progression."

However, before they could get to work on *A New Flame* there was a special moment for Simply Red when they made their live debut in Latin America in January 1988 at the Hollywood '88 Rock Festival in Sao Paulo, Brazil.

The head of WEA International's operations in Brazil was Andre Midani and while he watched their record sales increase and the radio play grow, he was still surprised at what happened next. "Nothing could have predicted the sound of over 60,000 people singing along with Simply Red."

"Seeing thousands of people in an audience is not daunting, I see it as very inviting. My view of that was formed long ago – when they see me on stage they want me to be a lion not a sheep; I go up there and want to involve them. If they've bothered to come then I'm gonna entertain them."

For Nicol, it also represented a turning point for Simply Red. "That was quite spectacular and being part of that festival kicked it off for Simply Red in the region. Brazil is not as American-influenced as the rest of Latin America and the tack was different there because they are a country that is susceptible to ballads."

After Brazil the band rested until late 1988 when they departed for 11 dates in Spain and Portugal, and it gave one very special friend and fan a chance to see the band again. Sheila had moved to Spain and welcomed the opportunity to see Mick for the first time since a gig at Manchester's Apollo Theatre a few years earlier when she had been "overwhelmed by his singing voice, his confidence and how great a performer he was".

The man she helped introduce to music 20 years earlier was now a star and in Valencia she had the chance to experience his new life-style. "We all went out for a pre-show dinner and drinks and I asked Michael when he was leaving for the show as time was getting on. He said that the audience were not going anywhere, and they'd wait even if he was a little bit late."

With that Mick apparently hailed a taxi, closely followed by Sheila and friends, and by the time they got to their seats, he was on stage and into the first number.

Life Tour, Wembley Arena, 1995

Meanwhile, Nick Levitt was busy preparing a tour for the new album and it involved working with both a design team and the band's management in order to come up with an overall plan for the shows. A tour's name and logo can come from an album's title and artwork if the imagery can be worked into the stage set and it was usually down to Mick, together with Elliot, to decide what worked and what didn't.

"Elliot was always very much part of it from the start and then Mick would get involved with the stage and the presentation and say what he liked and what didn't work for him. But his main focus is always the music and while some bands wrap themselves around the design aspect, it's the music that carries a Simply Red show," says Levitt.

After rehearsing the band, deciding how the set will run and how each song will be presented, Mick, according to Levitt, usually shows up for the first production rehearsals. "When we've got the whole show together, he'll stand back from it and maybe talk to the design team or the lighting crew but he doesn't have a huge involvement. Unless, of course, he doesn't like it and then we have to go and start again."

Levitt's brief also involves making it work for the people who have paid good money for the privilege of seeing Simply Red in concert. For him being practical means being able, when necessary, to put on a "great five-truck show" and avoiding the pitfalls of huge sets and designs that don't make any financial sense for anyone – band, management or fan.

"Mick doesn't want to cheat. He wants a really good show, a good-looking show. He wants to present something fantastic to the public but he doesn't want a show that distracts from the music. But," adds Levitt reassuringly, "he's also financially aware and doesn't want to go out on tour and lose money."

Planning a tour takes time, effort, teamwork and understanding. "I don't think I ever had to tell Mick that he couldn't do something from a design point of view, but in terms of logistics I have," explains Leviit. "I have to spell out the practicalities, that you can't get from A to B, you can't travel that route because of so and so. It doesn't matter who you are, everybody, including Mick, has to look at the budget so we all know and agree what we are trying to achieve."

Galbraith confirms Mick's commitment to the concept of touring and his overall control of events. "He always signs off on every stage set and is involved with all the projects and, since we came out of theatres, some of Simply Red's live shows have been ground-breaking and among the most innovative around."

Touring year after year helped Simply Red and the team understand their audience and make decisions about advertising and ticket pricing. Galbraith says that if he were allowed to place only one advert for a Simply Red tour he would

Top and Bottom: *Life* Tour, Wembley Arena, 1995

cut it in two and put half in the *Daily Mail* and half in *The Mail on Sunday*, and he knows that probably isn't what Mick would like to hear.

"I know Mick would like to think that his audience is perhaps younger and more left-field but it's not – it's middle England and predominantly female."

As one of the first bands to charge £40 a ticket for arenas – "We thought it was going to be an issue but it wasn't" says Galbraith – Simply Red very early on adopted a system of using the more lucrative tours to finance more exotic excursions.

"They took high earnings from UK and major European markets and used them to fund trips to places in the world where, in isolation, it wouldn't stack up financially," explains Galbraith, who is also charged with keeping things interesting. "I know why they go to weird and wonderful places – it's to keep Mick happy on the road. Just going round and round to the same places is soul-destroying and I know he loved going to South Africa and the trips to South America."

In fact it was in South America that Galbraith, Levitt and Dodd began to think that one of their best-laid plans had actually fallen apart. "We were staying at this hotel in Rio where they had a par three golf course," recounts Galbraith, "and then Mick, who doesn't play golf, decided to join us for a game... and he loved it.

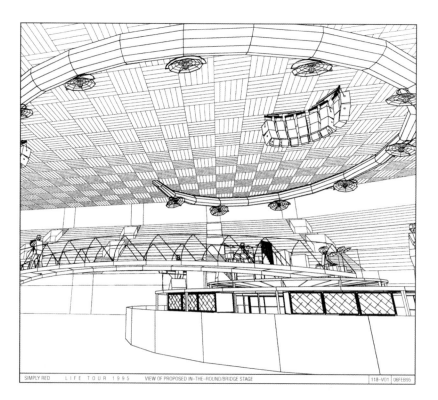

"There we were, thinking this was terrible because now we wouldn't be able to get away from Mick for the four hours or so when we played golf, because he was going to take it up as well. We decided we'd try and talk him out of it but, fortunately, although he was pretty good at it, he didn't take it up and he left us alone."

The move into bigger arena venues was a natural progression for Simply Red as they became ever more popular and successful. From October 1988 through to March 1990, the band's itinerary included over 140 shows as they travelled between the UK, Europe, North America, Japan, New Zealand and Australia.

Seeing Simply Red return Down Under for ten sell-out shows in Australia came as no surprise to Ikin but he knew that if things didn't work out the band would not be returning. "Travelling all the way to Australia and making it work financially means you need to fill in some dates along the way in Japan or South East Asia, where to be honest they didn't have huge record sales. We probably supported the tour there in order to get dates in Australasia where they always sold out and had good record sales."

While, understandably, he never went to Australia to see his son, Reg, oddly didn't go when he played nearer to home in Manchester or anywhere else in the UK

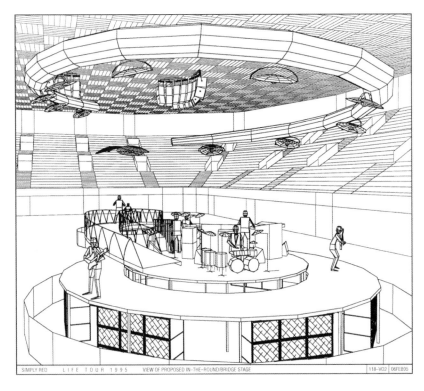

SIMPLY RED · LIFE TOUR 1995 · VIEW OF PROPOSED IN-THE-ROUND/BRIDGE STAGE · 118-V02 · 06FEB95

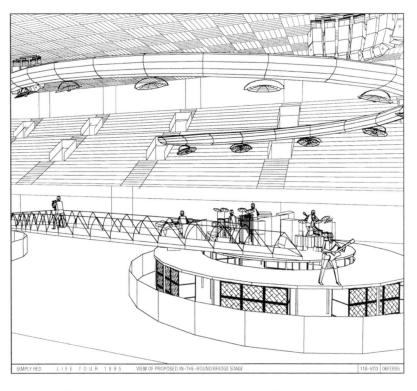

SIMPLY RED · LIFE TOUR 1995 · VIEW OF PROPOSED IN-THE-ROUND/BRIDGE STAGE · 118-V03 · 06FEB95

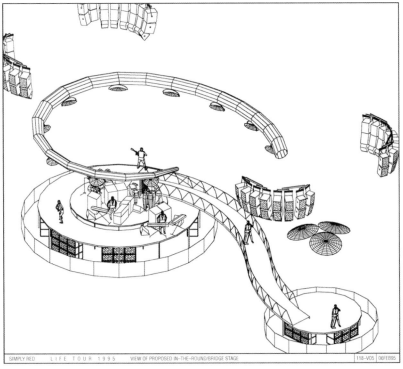

SIMPLY RED · LIFE TOUR 1995 · VIEW OF PROPOSED IN-THE-ROUND/BRIDGE STAGE · 118-V05 · 06FEB95

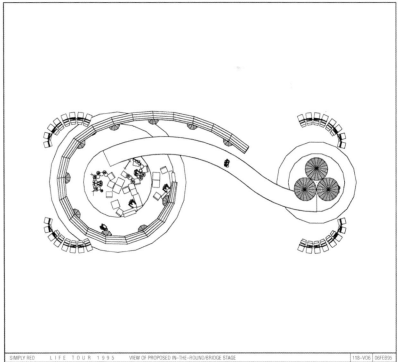

SIMPLY RED · LIFE TOUR 1995 · VIEW OF PROPOSED IN-THE-ROUND/BRIDGE STAGE · 118-V06 · 06FEB95

Mick and Quincy Jones, Montreux Jazz Festival,
June 1996

for that matter. However, he did make a trip to Spain to see the band in Barcelona at the start of the 1988 tour – and what he saw made him one very proud dad. "As we approached Barcelona in the car there were these Simply Red posters all over the place, and I realised then that he had 'arrived'. I got a feeling of great pride about that."

Wherever and whenever Simply Red appeared, one of the ongoing problems for Galbraith was getting the right support act for Mick and the band. "It is the one major difficulty with Simply Red. Mick wants contemporary and cutting-edge but bands like that don't always want to play with Simply Red so invariably we've gone for new and developing acts.

"I think the only time we had a name support was for an arena tour in the UK with Terence Trent D'Arby, which worked, but the support act always knows that Mick's fans are so avid and are there just to see Simply Red."

Anne-Marie Nicol was on the Simply Red/Trent D'Arby tour and recalls overhearing someone telling Mick that booking Trent D'Arby was "mad, he could blow you off stage." She heard Mick reply, "if he blows me off stage that's my problem, it means I'm not good enough."

Mick's huge workload in support of his records didn't go unnoticed at his record company and Max Hole, then a Warner UK executive, fully appreciated the efforts of his star act. "Mick worked really hard. He toured everywhere and regarded travelling as an adventure. He liked to travel, he liked different foods and he liked chasing girls! He was the perfect rock 'n' roll animal but he never got so out of it that he couldn't sing or do an interview, although sometimes you had to jump through a few hoops to get him out of bed in the morning."

One of the promotional trips to set things up in America for the *Stars* album involved a performance on the highly-rated Arsenio Hall show and it meant a first outing for the new band. Unfortunately the show wouldn't decide whether the band were expected to do one or two songs and the local backing singers hired for the show didn't make things any easier, according to original management assistant Bob Harding. "The two girls had been sent a cassette with two songs on it and when we did a run through for 'Something Got Me Started' one of the girls shouted, 'Hey we don't know this one, we only learned the other one.'"

At this point Harding was within range of what he describes as "one hell of a temper that you do not want to get on the wrong side of" as Mick demanded to know why the girls didn't know both songs. "I just wanted the ground to open up and swallow me until they said, 'We learn real quick' and they did – in about ten minutes they had the whole thing off. In the end we only did one song and of course it was the one they learned first, but that really wasn't the point."

Top: Filming the *Home Live in Sicily* DVD, Taormina, Sicily, 2003

Bottom: Band and crew on the *A New Flame* Tour

By constantly touring and playing hundreds of shows a year there will, by the laws of average, be days when it doesn't go exactly to plan, and Nick Levitt has experienced a few disasters. "The whole PA system went off in Zurich one night and Mick picked up an acoustic guitar and just played and sang while we all scrambled around getting the power back on. Other times we've had to take the whole band offstage because there is no power at all but only rarely have we had to cancel shows.

"We had part of the lighting rig come down in rehearsal and that was so dangerous we had to call off the show and other times trucks don't get through because of the weather, but nine times out of ten the show does go on."

If the 1991 album *Stars* was the biggest record in Simply Red's history, the tours that went with it also set new records. From the first dates in January 1992 through to the final show at Wembley Arena in December 1993, they set new standards for Simply Red with what Galbraith describes as three tours.

"We did a brief arena run, then we did stadiums and outdoor shows – known as one day internationals – and then we came back and did a major arena tour. The biggest shows they ever played were on the back of *Stars*."

"I am up for trying anything but I was never comfortable with stadiums. I just didn't want to play them because they were too big. We don't make rock music, we don't make sloganeering music, U2 belong there – they are anthemic. Our music is soul-jazz, it's more sophisticated and more intimate and it's designed for intimate settings.
My mission is to get the music across to people so I try and find methods of doing that. All I have is the music and my voice."

In fact, the 123 shows they played in 1992 – spread across 294 days – attracted a massive 1.4 million people around the world and included a new record for Sheffield Arena with 4 sold-out shows grossing £1.4 million.

For Nellie and her family, the band's show at Manchester's G-Mex arena in early 1992 holds special and personal memories. The concert took place not long after the death of Alf, Nellie's husband and Sheila's dad. At the end of the show, as an encore, Mick went back on stage carrying a stool and a guitar and said, "This is for Alf who is probably up there with Freddie (Mercury, who died at the end of 1991) watching tonight."

Sheila has never forgotten that moment. "He then went on to sing 'Holding Back The Years' which is my mother's favourite. We were all in tears and after the show when I thanked him for singing it for dad, he just said, 'He was worth it.'"

It was also an unexpected and moving moment for Nellie. "It was very, very emotional. Elliot's mum was sat behind me and she was emotional too.

Spirit of Life Tour, Wembley Arena, March 2000

I think everybody was. Nobody expected it, and I was thinking, 'I hope you're listening up there, Alf.'"

In fact, Nellie was a regular visitor backstage when Simply Red played shows in the Manchester area, and became something of an agony aunt to the band. "They all came up to me after the shows and talked about their girlfriends, lifestyles, their homes and that. They came and told me their troubles and problems."

The *Stars* tour saw the band play two fully-packed shows at the massive Wembley Stadium and sell 95,000 tickets in Manchester in a single weekend (before internet booking) which Galbraith believes is something that is not likely to be repeated. "It was a special moment in time for them and in my career as a promoter. We could do no wrong; we could have sold as many tickets as we wanted for Simply Red."

"When you have 9,000 people all singing along that's a great experience for the person singing. You've got 9,000 people being ridiculous too and you feel good about that. My ideal audience is between seven and fifteen thousand, indoors – that's what I love to play. Give me Wembley Arena, the NEC – I love 'em.

The open air places are a lot harder to get an atmosphere. The Lancashire Cricket Club is just a fantastic place which somehow has this old-fashioned club feel that makes you feel good. It was a lovely warm gig that and I have particularly fond memories of the groundsman worrying about his pitch – it was a great experience."

In fact the band's show in July 1992 at Old Trafford, the home of Lancashire County Cricket Club, was the best Simply Red show ever for Galbraith who has literally hundreds to choose from. "It was his home town but it stands out for other reasons too. It was the widest outdoor stage ever built – something like 300 feet wide – and the whole show was beyond amazing."

The extra-wide stage in fact provided the tour organisers with problems from Day One. In order to test-build the stage they needed a large area of flat tarmac and it turned out that the only available space was the car park at the NEC in Birmingham. With the stage built, it still had to be tested with a full run-through and this, according to Galbraith, proved to be a bonus for a bunch of fans. "The band did the run-through in the car park and by the time they finished there were about 3,000 people out on the streets around the NEC getting a free show."

Nick Levitt was the man charged with planning and designing the *Stars* show and it didn't start out as a success. "We designed a show, put it into production rehearsal and halfway through the designer came back and said, 'It's rubbish, we can't do this.'"

Renowned lighting designer Patrick Woodruffe was then brought in to sort things out and he produced a design incorporating the album's *Stars* theme.

Top: Ian Kirkham   Bottom: Kenji Suzuki

It became the biggest tour in Simply Red's history and in production terms it grew from a three or four truck job to a massive 12 to 15 trucker. The dates went from indoors at large arenas, including two dozen shows at Wembley and the NEC, to stadiums, with Old Trafford representing the first time a cricket ground had been used to host a rock show.

"It was a real challenge," says Levitt. "Mick was having to perform on a much bigger stage and to a lot bigger audience, with the challenge of keeping it intimate. At Wembley we played across the stadium rather than at one end and that brought the audience way in to meet us."

And those challenges had to be met all around the world as the *Stars* tour set off on its two-year joy-ride taking in places such as Tel Aviv, Jerusalem, Athens and Singapore for the first time. "We took the whole *Stars* show – lights and stage – around the world. For every show we got advance details of the venue, got all the technical drawings and overlaid our plans on those drawings to make sure it all worked before the tickets went on sale," explains Levitt, who moved up from stage manager to production manager before eventually becoming Simply Red's tour director.

Alongside sax and keyboard player Ian Kirkham on the *Stars* tour was new drummer Gota who was making his live debut with the band, and has a special reason for remembering at least one of the shows. "I had my birthday on that tour and at the NEC the whole audience – about 10,000 people – all sang 'Happy Birthday' to me, which was wonderful. The Brazil Carnival was also great and playing both Wembley Stadium and Arena were special moments for me. In New York, when we played in Central Park and started doing some tracks from *Stars*, the stars began to come out, which was incredible."

Despite playing to a capacity 6,000 audience in New York, America did not take to *Stars* and Simply Red's appeal was on the wane, which Anne-Marie Nicol felt had a major impact on Mick. "Despite his two number one hits in America, I think he was always depressed by the relative lack of success there. I told him that in order to break it and become really big he would have to spend time there and work it – go to places like Montana, to some hick radio station where you have to say, 'Hey guys you're great.'"

But that was not for Mick, who decided he didn't want to travel around middle America visiting tiny radio stations, doing in-store promotions and talking to people who didn't understand his accent.

Besides America, Gota's big regret was that during his time with the band his family never got to see him play live with Simply Red in his homeland of Japan, but he did the next best thing. "I did bring my mum to Hong Kong to see a show and that was very special to me."

Top: Wayne Stobbart   Bottom: Sarah Brown

For Kirkham the *Stars* tour holds a different memory. "That was when I remember it becoming tough for the first time. It seemed like we did ten weeks in Germany (actually it was just over two) and at that point it seemed like everybody was at each other's throats. Travelling on buses, seeing each other every day – it was all too much."

Even the change from smaller halls and theatres to vast stadiums went virtually unnoticed, according to Kirkham. "I don't specifically remember when it happened, but we would come back from playing a theatre in Europe one day to playing somewhere much bigger the next. The transition was so smooth that you had to stop yourself and say, 'Hang on we're at the Maracana Stadium in Brazil with over 80,000 people or Wembley Stadium or Old Trafford.' Then you think that it's all getting out of control."

"*Around the time of* Stars *and* Life *I thought it was getting beyond my control. It was all being too produced with me just being wheeled on. Sometimes I just see things and think the concept's gone way beyond me now. What I try to do now is say that I don't want gimmicks all around it. I want you to be creative in lighting us, we are the priority. Enhance what's there!*"

Any musician will tell you that constant touring and travelling, no matter how glamorous it may seem, will lead to the odd tantrum and Mick is no exception to the rule. At these times, Galbraith counts himself lucky to be just an observer rather in the firing line. "Thankfully I'm twice removed. There are Mick's people on the road who deal with my representative on the tour but we've still had our moments.

"He's a red-head and a fiery red-head on occasions," adds Galbraith, "but that was a phase. He has calmed down a lot over the years and in the main he's been a pleasure to work with."

After a year off, the band re-emerged for another round of touring from the end of 1995 through to the middle of 1996 in support of the *Life* album. They visited all the regular haunts with three dates in the United Arab Emirates as an added bonus, and once again Nick Levitt was there in the wings.

"At the start of the tour I do watch the whole of the show but then as it gets under way I just watch the start. I'm looking at the design mainly to see how it slots into the show. We change things throughout the tour to make sure it's exactly right."

But the tour director is careful not to get involved in areas that don't concern him... like the music. "That's not my area and I don't talk to Mick about it. But he plays around with the set all the time, changing the running order, and that in turn affects the lighting as he'll be cued with lights for entrances or certain songs. Overall he doesn't like being choreographed and there aren't loads of costume changes, so it's not too difficult."

Top: Dee Johnson   Bottom: Gota Yashiki

A show that was supposed to be one of the highlights of 1996 is remembered by Levitt for all the wrong reasons. Simply Red interrupted their European tour to play the Old Trafford soccer stadium at Euro '96 – the European football championships – where the band's 'We're In This Together' was the official theme.

"It was one of the worst load-ins I've been involved with. The weather was horrendous, we were playing in the round outdoors, which is a challenge, and because there was a match the night before, we couldn't get in until midnight and we were still working right up to show time."

With Woodruffe already on-board as lighting designer, another creative visionary was added soon after when Mark Fisher came on-board and between them the two men – most famously associated with the masterpieces that were Rolling Stones and Pink Floyd sets – quickly made a significant contribution to Simply Red's live work, according to Dodd, "Set designer Mark Fisher, with Woodruffe, played a huge role in presenting Simply Red to the world. I'll never forget how effective the figure of eight stage on the Life tour was, although all Mick will remember is that he had run about eight miles a night to make it work!"

After over a decade touring, Simply Red took another year out in 1997 as work began on the next new album and when they returned to the stage a year later it was London's small but legendary Lyceum Theatre which served to kick-start another international date sheet.

"The Lyceum shows on their own didn't stack up financially," explains Galbraith, so, despite sales of the DVD release of the shows, the band were soon back on the road. "We had to go out and play other shows and get a run-together that made financial sense."

In 1999 and 2000, with the release of *Blue* and *Love And The Russian Winter*, while they focussed on a regular European tour together with some prestigious UK venues, Simply Red also took the opportunity to plan a trip to South Africa for the first time, alongside their debuts in Mexico and Uruguay.

Even after this Mick was still keen to play new and untried venues, and the castles of England seemed to fit the bill. "Warwick Castle was exquisite, absolutely mind-bogglingly beautiful" recalls Galbraith, who puts Cardiff Castle and Haydock race course in the same special category.

While the special UK gigs were stealing all the headlines, Adrian Thrills was in Lisbon in March 2000 for a Simply Red show that he considers their best ever. "It was a warm evening in Lisbon, Mick was in a kind of dinner shirt with a dark jacket, and he just came across as being the consummate adult entertainer. It was just simply a memorable show."

Top: Tim Vine   Bottom: Mark Jaimes

Old Trafford, Manchester, 1993

After all the hard work involved with touring, there comes the need for some serious playtime and part of Levitt's job – apart from keeping Mick off the golf course – is keeping everybody happy while they are away from home.

South African safaris, pistol shooting, horse riding and go-karting have all been part of the touring itinerary and, in Levitt's book, they have an important role to play in life on the road. "For the smooth running of the tour it's important to pull everybody together. You pull the crew and the band together for meals and that's important for camaraderie. Sometimes people do want to be on their own and Mick joins in when he can, but he has to do promotion and rest his voice."

"On tour I shut up most of the time to protect my voice – they do actually shut me up sometimes, believe it or not. I shut up after shows and have to be quiet during the day, and when we're on the road I'm usually in my hotel room and don't speak to anybody. I tend to rest on tour. I don't speak in order to rest my voice which actually gets stronger as it goes on throughout the tour. I do a little bit of football and I've done all the sightseeing and we started to do go-karting."

Horse riding was one of the biggest risk areas and, while Levitt acknowledges that for most people it was great fun, "seeing horses run off with one of your band members is a bit of a worry." Keeping the star of the show out of trouble is another worry and while Mick has taken to a bit of horse riding, there is a worry about him skiing and parachuting. "You are asking for a cancellation," says Levitt who recalls that before he joined up, a Simply Red versus UB40 cricket match was a regular fixture while table tennis tournaments gave Fritz McIntyre the chance to wipe the floor with everybody.

But not surprisingly, when away from home a young man's thoughts turn to soccer in all its forms. "We had a five-a-side tournament going indoors all the way through the *Stars* tour but we broke Elliot's leg and I nobbled Heitor the guitar player. He was out of action for a while. He didn't miss any gigs but he didn't move about the stage very much," admits Levitt.

So from indoor five-a-side, Simply Red moved up to an 11-man football team made up of band and crew, and local promoters were asked to find opponents for games on the days off. "We've played some fantastic games around the world," explains Levitt, who cherishes one in Hungary in 1996. "We played a Ferencvaros Old Boys X1 and they slaughtered us, which wasn't surprising when we realised that they had two of the Hungarian international team that thrashed England 6-3 in1953."

With the release in 2003 of his new album *Home*, the first on his own label, Mick chose to do something that didn't make sense financially but fitted the bill musically. "It cost hundreds of thousands of pounds to do the week at

Top: Team shot, May 1993   Bottom: Post-match soundcheck

51

Simplified photoshoot at Fulham Town Hall,
April 2005

Ronnie Scott's to launch *Home*," says Galbraith, "and I thought they were all mad but as a set-up for the record it was perfect."

The idea of using Ronnie Scott's for a launch came initially from Mick's PR consultant Moira Bellas but once Mick had taken it on board, it continued to grow and even current co-manager Ian Grenfell admits it got out of hand.

"It was ridiculous. It cost an obscene amount of money but I've always believed that if something is right, and that good things will come from it, then you've got to do it almost whatever the cost. Rationally it made no sense, but as soon as Moira came up with the idea we knew it was right. A residency, starting at 6.30 in the evening meant you got all the people down who hadn't played a Simply Red record for ages and re-introduced them to the band. We knew that hearing Mick sing in that sort of environment was going to be very special."

Mick's music publisher Peter Reichardt was also a supporter of the idea and appreciates exactly what it did for Simply Red. "It put Mick back on the front page of the music business and that word-of-mouth thing started up about how good it was and it set it all off on the right path."

Adrian Thrills was also in the audience at London's most famous jazz club and he agrees that it worked. "Mick can work a small smoky club as well as anyone but I have to say that his ideal concert is open air, early evening with about 2,000 to 3,000 people – then he really is in his element. I don't think he does the really big venues as well as U2 or Robbie Williams who just get better the bigger the venue."

In support of the important new album, Simply Red spent most of 2003 on the road playing over 100 dates in ten months, visiting the UK, Europe, United Arab Emirates, South Africa, Brazil and North America along the way.

"The best gigs we've done so far were in Liverpool and New York on the Home tour with this new band – phenomenal. No doubt, they have been the best ever. New York was unbelievable and the atmosphere in Liverpool in this sort of circus tent near the dock was just fantastic. And when we were on tour there was a brilliant ambience between all the band members, a really great atmosphere that lasted through a very difficult tour of over 100 shows that went backwards and forwards across time zones. It's a real challenge on the body to do shows as well as the travelling, but everybody was in really good spirits."

With a year's touring behind them, the band had 2004 off but planning for the next round of concerts was already underway and Nick Levitt is always confident that, even after 18 months off the road, Mick comes back with his batteries re-charged. "Once he walks in for band rehearsals he'll be there, he loves performing."

Filming *Cuba!* DVD, El Gran Teatro, Havana,
Cuba, 2005

In 2005 Mick returned to one of his favourite UK music venues – London's Albert Hall. Since his shows there in 1989 it remained a special place even though, as Levitt admits, it has its drawbacks. "It's a very difficult place to work and financially it's not great as it's very expensive, but Mick wanted somewhere special, and the nights at the Albert Hall were great for the fans and much nicer than just doing another Wembley."

"I hope people realise that we try to be as adventurous as we can but you can only be in one place at one time. The tours are scheduled around a whole lot of factors like stadium availability and it has to make sense financially. There are a lot of places I'd like to go to – Moscow for one – and I tell people that and hope they'll give me one or two nice surprises. That's one area I leave to promoters and tour organisers. I just give them a time zone. I'll say that I'm available from September to August next year – do your worst!"

Under Grenfell's guidance, Simply Red continued their touring schedule in 2005 and 2006, again as part of a well co-ordinated campaign in support of an album, but he admits that the time has come for change. "It's more likely that in future we'll do just 30 dates at a time rather then the massive 120-date tours they did in the past. We'll still try to get to all the places we've been to before but just not as part of a year-long world tour."

Twenty years after he started working with Simply Red, Galbraith is still a fan and even today has what he calls "those hairs on the back of the neck moments" when he sees the current band at work. "The line-up now is probably the best band Mick has ever had and it never ceases to amaze me that he can be that good live."

As a latecomer to the world of Simply Red, music arranger Simon Hale's first experience of working on stage with Mick and the band came in Cuba, and he was immediately impressed with the main man's grasp of the situation.

"After the first night there was a set change as Mick judged how the audience had reacted to the show," recalls Hale. Despite Cuba's closeness to Jamaica, the band's reggae songs had not connected with the audience and Mick responded without hesitation.

"He knew what was happening so he changed it and he was right. He is one of those focussed artists who still cares about the music," is Hale's explanation.

Simply Red's 2006 summer concerts at major UK venues such as Leeds Castle and Blicking Hall were followed by over a month of touring Europe, and plans for the new 2007 album release include another series of dates which means that Mick and his band of troubadours have, since 1984, only missed out five years when they did not play any live gigs.

The strain of constantly touring, in addition to making records and doing promotional work, is not lost on Dodd who has watched Mick work at his chosen profession for over two decades. "It's very difficult to put yourself through the sausage machine in this business year after year – ultimately it's soul destroying. For me he's first and foremost a great singer and as long as he chooses to continue performing there will always be an audience out there for him."

But with an eye to the future Dodd offers Mick a get-out clause. "Yes, he's a great performer but he's also an excellent chef – absolutely superb – so if it all goes horribly wrong he can always go into the restaurant business or tend his vines in Italy."

"I still love performing on stage but since September 11 the whole travelling thing has taken on a different set of connotations. It's very stressful and it's wearing me down a bit. I don't see me doing it in my sixties and I really admire the Rolling Stones, who I think are amazing, but I just don't see how I'm going to do that. I look at someone like Keith Richards and that's what he does and he does it better than anyone else in the world, so why would he want to stop.

I still love making music and I'll always make music but the amount of time we have to devote to going out on the road could maybe take up to six months of the year, and because I have other interests in my life I just don't see how I'm going to do that in future."

01 Kevin Robinson *Trumpet & Flute*
02 Sarah Brown *Backing Vocals*
03 Pete Lewinson *Drums*
04 Dee Johnson *Backing Vocals*
05 Chris De Margary *Flute & Saxophone*
06 John Johnson *Trombone & Percussion*
07 Kenji Suzuki *Guitar*
08 Steve Lewinson *Bass Guitar*
09 Mick Hucknall *Vocals*
10 Dave Clayton *Keyboards*
11 Ian Kirkham *MD, Saxophone & Keyboards*

01	02	03
04	05	06
07	08	09
10	11	

WE'RE IN THIS TOGETHER

WE'RE IN THIS TOGETHER

"I first established myself musically in 1984 when we started Simply Red."

Simply Red, after months spent searching for a new identity, finally emerged into a world of pop music dominated by the prancing and preening of modern romantics Duran Duran and Spandau Ballet, Culture Club's cross-dressing singer Boy George, and Michael Jackson's slickest moves.

The band that was launched in 1983 as Ghost Shirt featured Mick alongside guitarist Dave Rowbotham, bassist Tony Doyle, Chris Joyce on drums and Kate Crabtree on keyboards. By the end of the year they had become World Service with Dave Fryman (guitar), Mog (bass), Eddie Sherwood (drums) and Ojo (trumpet) joining Mick but that didn't last long and, perhaps as a sign of things to come, they experimented with Red and the Dancing Dead, All Red and Just Red.

One man who watched all these comings and goings with more than a passing interest was Elliot Rashman who, in his capacity as entertainment manager at the University of Manchester Institute of Science and Technology (UMIST), had once booked the Frantic Elevators and had never forgotten the singer. Hearing Mick sing during the band's sound check in the college bar set the seal on his future career. He was going to manage and steer this kid with the astonishing voice towards greatness.

"I didn't realise my voice was anything special until I was about 23. By then I'd been able to hit a lot of high notes and a lot of low notes which meant that I could do whatever I wanted... to choose a melodic note or anything like that. That's when you start thinking, 'Hang on a minute, I can do this.'"

With Rashman's help Mick began to put together the band that was to become Simply Red. The name came from the band's new manager, who got his way despite protests from his protégé.

"It would have been in late 1984 when we first formed Simply Red. Elliot was responsible for the Simply. Initially I wanted to call the band Red and he would say,

Early line-up of Simply Red

'What just Red?' and I'd say, 'Yeah, just Red'. So he said why don't you call it Simply Red, which I thought was ridiculous. I said that people would end up dropping the Simply and just call us Red. But I was wrong and he was right."

While Mick was dj-ing at Manchester Poly, courtesy of Rashman, the band were also beginning to pick up regular work around the Manchester area including gigs at the Poly which were also booked by Rashman, who got his band to play for free.

Simply Red now consisted of Fryman alongside ex-Mothmen drummer Joyce, Tony Bowers (bass), Fritz McIntyre (keyboards) and Tim Kellet (horns). It was no coincidence that Bowers and Joyce were friends of Rashman.

As the band built up a local following, so the third member of the team came in to play alongside Mick and Rashman. Andy Dodd was a promoter specialising in booking jazz acts at the Band On The Wall club, but after hiring Simply Red he was invited to bring his financial acumen into the emerging So What Arts operation which had been created to oversee the business of Simply Red.

As two promoters who were both operating in and around Manchester, Rashman and Dodd, not surprisingly, had crossed paths and developed what Dodd describes as "a mutual admiration for our promotional activities."

In fact it was Rashman who alerted Dodd to Mick while he was still fronting the Frantic Elevators. "I had heard them rehearse a few times and I didn't get it, it didn't appeal to me at all." But that all changed for Dodd, who had been in Manchester for six years and was busy promoting concerts and festivals, when he stepped into a Simply Red gig at Manchester Poly in April 1984.

"There were only a couple of hundred people there," recounts Dodd, "and when Mick sang I thought 'God this guy's got the voice of an angel.' It was so powerful and what really got me was his interpretation of Talking Heads' 'Heaven'."

Although he wasn't at any of those early Simply Red gigs, band leader and TV presenter Jools Holland has both worked with and watched Mick Hucknall perform and offers a professional musician's assessment of what he's heard. "Not a lot of people realise that he has a bass voice and he's very much in the mould of singers like Frank Sinatra and Tom Jones. Lots of people can hit the high notes but they can't reach the bass notes and that's what gives Mick's voice its tone and makes it so amazing."

In the wake of seeing Simply Red for the first time, Dodd and Rashman maintained a regular dialogue and, according to Dodd, it was in Sheffield in December 1984 when he and Rashman "conspired to form the management company." Having made their decision to work together there was a surprise waiting for them on their return to Manchester. "The night was capped off by

Top: Chris Joyce   Bottom: Fritz McIntyre

us getting back to Manchester Poly to find Elliot's car mysteriously in flames outside the building," explains Dodd, adding, "I thought there was a certain dangerous magic about it and I liked that."

"Andy came in pretty soon after Elliot. He was very much around the same scene, he was involved in promotion around the north and I always liked him, He just gradually got involved and booked us for a couple of gigs and then Elliot brought him in to handle the financial side of things."

Not surprisingly, Mick's dad Reg was high on Rashman's visitors list as he plotted the route for Simply Red's road to success. "I first met Elliot on a Sunday afternoon when he drove up in a white Polytechnic van and told me how brilliant Mick was and how he was going to change the world. And of course I suppose they did, but I took it all with a pinch of salt back then."

Rashman also shared his conviction and confidence in Mick and Simply Red with Nellie during a visit to her home. "Elliot had this old banger he used to ride around in and he said to me, 'We are going to be rich one day and Mick's going to have a big house and so am I.' He used to say that with Mick's voice they'd both be rich."

Bob Harding, who runs Mick's Blood & Fire reggae operation, first came across Rashman and Dodd in the late 1970s when he was in The Mothmen with both Bowers and Joyce. It turned out that somewhere along the way Rashman had become the band's manager and now Harding was a regular at the Poly on Mick's weekly Black Rhythm nights.

Sitting on the sidelines also gave Harding an interesting view of what was developing with Rashman and Dodd. "It's true that Elliot brought Andy in because he needed someone to cover the business side of it, as Elliot was more interested in the creative side of things. But that's not to say that Andy didn't have an input as well, it was just that Elliot was the more forceful of the two."

No matter how they structured their working day, there was no doubting the fact that Dodd and Rashman shared the same vision for their new act. "I definitely felt that Simply Red, and specifically Mick, had immense potential and great power and energy," explains Dodd who also saw something special in the singer. "Right from the beginning he exuded a burning ambition that was unassailable... it's something that all the great artists have."

Music journalist Thrills recalls his first meeting with Mick in those early days when he combined playing records with fronting his new band. "He was living in a pretty squalid flat in Whalley Range and he was dj-ing at the Poly but I knew he was one of us, a real music fan. I spent a couple of days with him. We went down the pub and then back to his place where he'd just play music and then we'd talk music long into the night – he just loved music."

Top: Tim Kellett   Bottom: Tony Bowers

Simply Red's gigs in the last quarter of 1984 took them to Hebden Bridge, Manchester, Bedford and Sheffield before they ventured south of Watford for the first time to play at Goldsmith's College in London in January 1985. Their shows were beginning to get noticed and record company A&R (artist and repertoire) people were asking for their names to be put on the door. As the crowds grew, so did the interest, and one of the most interested parties was Saul Galpern from the newly-formed Elektra Records UK.

Elektra was a revered American record label which, in the years since it was started in 1950, had launched the careers of artists such as Judy Collins, Love, The Doors, Bread, the Eagles and Joni Mitchell. In February 1985, its American president Bob Krasnow opened a UK office and put former Arista label manager Simon Potts in charge with his fellow ex-Arista man Galpern on the staff.

In the week his new label opened, Potts told the world, "I intend to sign acts that move with instinct and taste," but it was Galpern who got to travel up and down the country searching for new acts. One of his trips took him to Manchester in search of a new band that was starting to turn a few heads.

"I went to the Poly to see Elliot and told him I wanted to get hold of this band called James. He gave me their details straightaway but then said, 'By the way I've got something for you, something really, really exciting.'"

London based A&R men are by their very nature a sceptical bunch and Galpern was no exception, but he was won over by the passion Rashman showed for his new act. "He said they were called Simply Red and that no one had heard them. He promised to send me a tape of some tracks they were working on and I thought nothing more of it until the tape arrived a few days later," recalls Galpern.

"I put it on and I couldn't believe what I was hearing. Even though it wasn't coming from a musical school I was brought up with, all I was hearing was this guy who had the most amazing voice I'd ever heard."

The cassette Rashman sent to Galpern contained versions of 'Holding Back The Years' and 'Sad Old Red' plus a cover of Al Green's 'Love And Happiness' but it was enough to make the Elektra man sit up and take notice. "It was so incredible. I was so excited by it. Obviously the band sounded ropey, it was very basic, very sparse as though it had been done on a cassette in a rehearsal room, but the voice and the songs just shone through."

But for all his excitement and enthusiasm, Galpern still had to persuade his boss that signing Simply Red was the right thing to do – and it wasn't that easy. "Simon didn't take much notice at first. I don't think he got it in the beginning," says Galpern, who was aware that the legendary Seymour Stein and Sire Records were sniffing around. He'd also heard that London, Island and CBS were interested.

Top: Elliot Rashman and Mick signing record deal with Simon Potts, Elektra UK

"Elliot met Simon Potts and Saul Galpern and then Saul just kept contacting us. We'd had an offer earlier, interestingly from Seymour Stein who had discovered and signed Madonna. At the time he was telling us, 'I've got this girl Madonna, she's going to be a huge star,' and he was right. I always had a great deal of respect for Seymour, he's got a great nose for music.

I knew Elektra was part of the American Warner company and we'd had it explained to us that it was a satellite of the company and it was separate to the WEA UK outfit. I think we went with it because Simon and Saul were charmers and were also prepared to give us a higher percentage as opposed to a high advance which we didn't want."

In fact, WEA executive Hole was among those who went along to cast an expert's eye over Simply Red. Together with Rob Dickins (MD of WEA UK) and Moira Bellas (head of press), he went to a gig in North London to see the unsigned Simply Red, but came away unconvinced. "I remember our overall feeling was, 'Great singer but no songs,' so we definitely passed, although Moira thought they had something."

Confirming that her two colleagues were "very unimpressed" with the early Simply Red, Bellas adds, "I was the only person who saw any potential. Mick's voice was amazing, I loved the songs and thought he was a star."

Armed with his vision of turning Elektra into a British Motown that would be home to the new UK soul movement, Galpern persuaded Potts that he needed to see Simply Red on stage. Together they made their way to Manchester's Tropicana in November 1984 and the journey turned into a revelation. "It was on the drive up to Manchester that I put the demo cassette on and suddenly Simon said, 'That's a fucking smash'. I said, 'I told you so' and just hoped that we weren't too late, because this was six or seven weeks after I had first got the tape."

The enthusiasm of Potts and Galpern, combined with a degree of charm, an understanding of what Simply Red were about musically and the fact that they were deadly serious, convinced the Simply Red camp that Elektra should be their new musical home.

"Actually signing was a difficult time for me. I'd been on the dole for four years and my psychology really was that in most people's eyes I was pretty worthless. Then all of sudden you get people hanging on every word you say and you start getting criticised when you do interviews or meet people in the industry.

Initially your reaction is to become very defensive but like a wounded animal you start lashing out as opposed to retaining any sense of reason. When you are being wound up by an emotive manager – and I think Elliot would admit himself that he was more emotional than reasoned in some cases – then you go the same way. Then the band went the same way and all this energy was firing around and we just kept rolling along in this way – which wasn't such a bad way at the time."

Mick and Tony Bowers

Mick, Lamont Dozier and Stewart Levine

Hole acknowledges that Galpern was the driving force behind the band signing to Elektra but never saw the deal as any sort of an embarrassment, although there were issues. "I wasn't particularly savvy in those days but I don't think Rob Dickins liked the fact that Elektra had an A&R office in the UK. There was political hassle because we provided the marketing and promotion services to Elektra Records, so there was always a bit of tension."

Signing directly to an American-owned label based in the UK – "not something I'd ever advise anyone to do" says Dodd – brought with it a host of strange contractual issues for Dodd and Rashman as they coped with a hectic first year during which Simply Red went from rank outsiders to fancied runners fast approaching the front of the race.

Concerned that the focus of attention and record company interest should rest on the shoulders of the band's young singer, Rashman, Dodd and Mick were anxious to ensure that everybody understood their vision of Simply Red. People had to see Mick as Simply Red with a collection of musicians who would appear with him on stage and in videos.

This made perfect sense to the people at Elektra and Potts and Galpern soon concluded the deal which, according to Galpern, didn't rank as being particularly expensive. "I remember it being £60,000 plus costs for five albums."

With the deal done, Reg went over to Didsbury – where the new So What Arts operation was now based in a rented house – for dinner and perhaps the chance to talk to Rashman about what he had in store for his son. "I went up on my bike and they put on a nice spread for me but Elliot was late getting back. Then when he arrived he wanted a shower and I couldn't wait any longer because I hadn't got any lights on my bike and had to get back before it got dark."

Although he didn't get the chance to discuss career development, Reg wasn't at all unhappy with what he saw. "I could see things were going well, they were very busy and were full of it. I could see things were OK."

With plenty of live dates in the diary, everyone's attention soon turned to making the first record to be released by the new Simply Red on their new label, and Galpern remembers it all being a reasonably democratic process. "It was a pretty fair mixture of Mick's ideas and our thoughts. We did discuss bringing in Alex Sadkin to produce the first album, which I thought made a lot of sense, but they wanted to use Stewart Levine because of his track record."

New Yorker Levine's work with Womack & Womack, the Crusaders and Sly Stone were among the reasons he had registered on Mick's radar and made him the band's first choice to produce their debut album in Holland and London's RAK Studios.

In fact, Levine's first introduction to the band was in January 1985 on the back of meeting up with Elektra UK boss Potts in the bathroom of Elektra chairman Bob Krasnow's London hotel room during a Super Bowl party.

"I didn't really know him but he asked me if I wanted to hear this band he'd signed. Back then, everybody was giving me tapes of bands. This was a chance to see a band perform live so I agreed to go with him."

After watching the show at Goldsmith's College, Levine went backstage to hook up and talk music with the band's singer. "We had a great deal in common and he was one of the very few people who knew of an album called *Ain't But One Way* that I'd done with Sly Stone. Mick was fascinated by it and Elliot told me later that, more than anything else, this was what made him want to work with me."

Despite their love of music and appreciation of each other's talents, it wasn't all mutual back-slapping that night, as Levine recalls. "I came right out and told him that I didn't like his band. I quite liked the rhythm section but the horn section was fucking horrible and looked like an old R&B soul revue.

"But he played the song 'Picture Book' that night and that killed me – that was it for me, that's what hooked me."

After the gig Levine was driven home by Potts and recalls that, as he got out of the car, he told the Elektra man exactly what he thought. "I didn't hide my feelings. I said I thought this guy was a killer singer but the band had problems and the repertoire, for the most part, was shit, but there was something magical about him."

Encouraged by Levine's enthusiasm for both Mick's singing and his charisma, Potts confessed to the American producer that he didn't think he would be able to afford him in view of his usual producer's royalty rate. "He said, 'I know you're a four point producer and I don't think I can do that.' Then he said he'd try to work it out."

Work it out they did, and Levine came on board to make an album that Galpern was happy with both in terms of process and outcome. "It all happened quite smoothly with just the usual give-and-take about tracks and running order."

Elektra set up 'Money's Too Tight To Mention' as the debut single in June 1985. It peaked at number 13 in the UK and over the next fifteen months, four more singles plus the album *Picture Book* entered the UK charts, made a significant impression around Europe and broke new ground in America.

The first Elektra Simply Red press biography in October 1985 quoted Mick as describing the band's debut release as "a great song" before adding, "but it's just the beginning." He went on to explain that his group were not revivalists. "America can be my influence but I'm fundamentally Mancunian."

Still not quite sure where his son's career was heading, Reg finally became convinced when he heard the song that was to become the band's debut single. "When I heard 'Money's Too Tight' I was dumbfounded. I heard it first as a demo on a little tape player – before it had been produced – and I was astounded, really impressed."

Stefano Senardi, head of international at Warner Music Italy, had heard the same demo of the first Simply Red record and was equally excited. "I asked Elektra for permission to release it immediately because there was an important TV show we could get it on."

Without the benefit of the early Elektra biog, any photos of the artist or even the parts to manufacture the single, Senardi gave the tape to the major Italian radio stations which immediately began playlisting the track. "I had no information and I thought it was by a black female singer. Then two weeks later I found out it was a band led by a singer called Mick Hucknall but I was still right about the strength and beauty of the song."

Producer Levine was equally convinced of the quality of the debut single that he had helped craft into a finished product. "It was a brilliant choice. I believe records are moments in time because they're snapshots of what's going on at that moment. This was a dance record and it was timely because Mick changed the lyrics to sing about Ronnie Reagan and Margaret Thatcher."

In fact, Mick's plans for the video originally included using puppets of the two political leaders from television's *Spitting Image* in the clip and in an early interview with *Smash Hits* he explained his reasons. "They are a threat to my class. They're obscene and vile and I wanted to have this thing in the video where they were having dinner and eating money. But it turned out (the puppets) were too expensive to hire."

Then 'Holding Back The Years' – the song written in Mick's bedroom in Denton that so upset his father – followed its initial lowly chart placing of 51 by storming back and ending up at number two. At the same time *Picture Book* also peaked just one off the top spot but raced to number 16 in the US where 'Holding Back The Years' reached the coveted number 1 position in July 1986. The album, which soon passed the one million sales mark, was also logged as one of the world's top five bestselling albums of the year.

"Having a US number one with 'Holding Back The Years' was phenomenal. It was bizarre really. We were still in digs in Didsbury and I was there one night when Elliot gets a phone call and then says, 'Oh you're number one in America' and I said, 'OK'. We opened some champagne and that was it. It just happened so quick, it grew into this monster in America and then the UK latched on to it again."

With his new-found fame, Mick became something of an enigma to people in Manchester who had watched him develop from the Frantic Elevators and

dj-ing to an international pop star. "For a while Mick walked around town with a hat and cane and people did have a pop at him and say, 'What a prat, this is Manchester not Hollywood, who does he think he is?' but it never fazed him," recounts former journalist Andy Spinoza.

"Just after *Picture Book* I was waiting for a bus and Mick was walking down Upper Chorlton Road like he was still a student and he came and waited for the bus with me. He was a bit of a superstar by then but he was still getting the bus."

Spinoza recalls that he once quoted somebody in an article he wrote for the *Manchester Evening News* who said that Mick didn't need a minder because, "He just walks round town and can handle himself and while he has the confidence and perhaps arrogance of a superstar, he doesn't have all the absurd trappings."

As the man who instigated the signing of Simply Red to Elektra, it was part of Galpern's job to encourage his colleagues at the head office in New York to take this new British band seriously – and it wasn't always easy. "There was always the potential for a clash between Elektra UK and the US people and there was some resentment about this white British soul band taking their music back to America."

In fact, despite their Englishness, when 'Holding Back The Years' came out, Simply Red were seen and heard by many in America as a local band with a black singer. Despite this, Galpern made a rash prediction. "Actually the Elektra people in America seemed quite positive about Simply Red but there were a few raised eyebrows when I told them 'Holding Back The Years' was going to be a US number one hit record."

One of the people involved with the first Simply Red records released in America in 1985 was Elektra's Barbaris, who worked specifically with TV and black music magazines. She recalls that the band's records came out at a time when the amalgamation of pop and R&B was at its height thanks to artists such as Lionel Richie, Billy Ocean and Midnight Star.

"Mick sat right in there as one of the most exciting new artists of the year but at the start there was some confusion. When we sent the record to radio they thought he was a black woman. Then they saw what he looked like – a bit of a punk – and he had this beautiful voice."

According to Barbaris, Mick's knowledge of American pop culture and US politics plus the fact that he used his lyrics to get across the odd political point worked in his favour. "Back then the media liked the fact that he was a bit outspoken and, as a result, he got great press."

When it was first released in the UK in November 1985, 'Holding Back The Years' was reviewed by the UK music industry's 'bible' *Music Week* and

its advice to retailers and broadcasters was that it was "a moody, swaying number that deserves plenty of exposure".

The more the song was heard, the more the lyrics were analysed and two lines in 'Holding Back The Years' – "Hoping for the arms of mater/ Get to meet her sooner or later" – set tongues wagging as people speculated that it was a song written about Mick's relationship with his mother.

Reg is adamant it wasn't but was concerned about the effect it might have. "That idea was a load of crap and I told Mick as soon as I heard it that she was bound to try and get in touch when she heard those lines. I thought it was a bit naughty, but to my way of thinking they were just words that didn't mean anything in particular. And I think in Mick's mind they were just words that went with the song, you know, fitted with the chorus."

Arriving back in Manchester as Simply Red enjoyed this initial burst of success was Bob Harding, who turned out be the proverbial right person in the right place at the right time. "When I came back the whole thing was taking off and Andy and Elliot wanted somebody to cover the office and answer the phones while they were out. As a result I became So What's first employee." He was soon to be joined by Lindy Everton who remained with the company until 2001.

As things got bigger so more people were recruited and eventually new offices were needed for the expanding So What operation, but Harding remembers that they were still in their original cramped offices when news of the band's major success in America filtered through. "Mick came in and started writing 1 on all the equipment in the office with a permanent marker pen – and all the stuff was leased."

"At the time Elliot was very, very sharp. He was totally into it to the point where I wanted him to get more sleep. I felt he was obsessing about it and when it started to affect his health that was crazy. He was up all night dealing with America and Australia to make sure these albums happened all over the world. It was amazing.

Elliot and Max Hole behaved in an intelligent way together and I'm sure they persuaded me to do a lot of things."

Meanwhile, Down Under in Australia, Peter Ikin heard the first records from Simply Red and was in for a surprise when he delved a little deeper. "The first time I heard them I thought they were an American soul band," he recalls. "This was because most of the music selling in Australia then was American and as Warners was an American company and had so many US acts, you began to assume everything came from America. And their sound was very much more American than British."

Reporting on all this first-time success, Thrills encountered problems of his own at *NME* where, he openly acknowledges, they were wary of artists who were successful and made pop records. "At that time *NME* revelled in being a bit

Left: Clockwise: Sylvan Richardson,
Tim Kellett, Chris Joyce, Fritz McIntyre,
Mick and Tony Bowers, Italy 1984

Top: Tony Bowers and Mick

Bottom: Chris Joyce

underground and there were a lot of people at the paper who were indifferent about Simply Red because it wasn't leftfield or indie or arty enough."

For Thrills, however, Simply Red represented something he had been waiting a long time to hear. "They were the perfect band for me and summed up everything I wanted music to say to me. It was British, it had good songs but it had a real American funk soul groove and it was political as well."

Being senior staff writer at NME and then features editor gave Thrills the chance to make sure Simply Red got space in the paper "despite opposition from within the ranks." He looks back on those times and assesses that Mick's uneasy relationship with NME had its roots in his own outspokenness.

"There were a lot of bands around – Specials, UB40, Simply Red – who had a kind of spirit but Mick was perhaps not too doctrinaire left-wing or preachy. More socially aware than political with a capital P, but I still got stick when I wrote about Mick and U2," explains Thrills. "Bono and Mick were both deemed a pain in the arse and certain rock journalists, perhaps because they have big egos themselves, didn't like these big, loud-mouthed people who had strong and outspoken views."

The important thing for Thrills was that Simply Red communicated with their audience through their music, but he acknowledges that some people weren't always on the same wavelength. "Some of the London media, the hipsters and the socialites had a problem with Mick because they didn't really understand where he came from. They saw this guy in the videos or up on stage and were thinking that he was maybe a bit less substantial than he was."

For Bellas, who got Mick on to the front cover of the influential Face magazine, life as Simply Red's PR was never dull. "Mick was always very opinionated but he was more interesting then a lot of pop stars because he had views about things other than music and was prepared to talk about them."

With his first hits under his belt and a full date sheet stretching from Glasgow to San Francisco and Milan to Vancouver, Mick began to focus on the all-important second album which was destined to be released on a new label

Just eight months after opening, and with label boss Krasnow's claim that it was "the most exciting thing to happen to Elektra" still ringing in people's ears, the operation based in north London's Camden district closed.

The closure didn't come as a complete surprise to Galpern, who had begun to hear rumours during a visit to a New Music seminar in New York. "A lawyer told me that there were problems with Elektra UK and people wanted to shut it down. I didn't quite know how it all worked back then but when I got back to England I was told there was an issue and that there was some political thing going on.

"It could have been to do with overheads and funding or maybe clashing with the Warner UK operation but I never really knew why it was closed."

Dear All, the first thing I do when I get back make a curry
what do you want me to say? A spicy one!
I'm homesick that's what.
I'm actually writing from New York.
I met Robert Mitchum today who looks fantastic!

SO WHAT
48 PRINCESS ST
MANCHESTER
ENGLAND.

NEW YORK, N.Y. 100
PM
18 NOV
1987

INCLUDE YOUR
APT #
BETTER SERVICE

POST CARD

USA 22

S-135
SAN FRANCISCO
The beautiful Oakland Bay Bridge sparkles on a
crystal clear night with San Francisco in the distance.
Photo by Mike Yuschenkoff

© 1986 Smith Novelty Co., 460 Ninth St.
San Francisco, California

Printed in Australia by Colorscans

According to Dodd, Galpern's boss got the word first-hand during a trip to New York to try and persuade Krasnow to increase the support for Simply Red. "You had this remarkable situation where Simon Potts was convinced the project was going to explode. He went to America to see Krasnow and get him to double the promotional budget, only to be told they were winding up the London office and that Potts was out of a job. That left us with a real problem."

"Early on there were mutual suggestions between us and Elektra. There were ideas that came from them that we had to swallow even though we didn't like them but realised after that they were right. I didn't think they were doing such a bad job, we were kinda rolling along quite nicely and then Bob Krasnow wielded the axe and Simon Potts' head rolled. Then Elliot started talking to Warners – Rob Dickins, Max Hole and Moira Bellas – and we gradually cut a deal where we came under the WEA umbrella. If Rob and Max thought early on that I had a great voice but no songs then they could have been right at the time."

Elektra closed in January 1986 and as a result Simply Red, with their first album still out there and with three chart singles to their credit, were switched to the company that had passed on them two years earlier. "When Elektra UK closed, Rob Dickins did a deal whereby WEA UK joint-ventured the album and WEA UK took over the contract from Elektra Records," explains Hole, who took up the baton for Mick and his band with the release of 'Jericho'.

"Mick and Elliot fell out with Krasnow after he closed the UK operation because of financial constraints and I became their A&R man in early 1986 and after 'Jericho' missed we all decided to re-release 'Holding Back The Years'," adds Hole. "It was a hit, got the first album alive again and I got off to a good start with everybody."

During the making of *Picture Book* the band experienced their first change in personnel when guitarist Fryman was replaced by the more experienced Sylvan Richardson. In addition to the six piece line-up, vocalist Janette Sewell and horn player Ian Kirkham were recruited as the band prepared for the all-important second album.

Kirham arrived on the scene courtesy of sax player Ian Dickson, who had played on *Picture Book*. Anxious to return to music college, Dickson tipped off Kirkham that there might be a chance for some work with Simply Red, a band he had heard of but never seen.

"I was told that this new band had done a version of 'Money's Too Tight To Mention' and I couldn't believe somebody had covered it, but when I heard it I thought, 'Yeah great'. Then I saw a video of 'Holding Back The Years' and that got me hooked straight away."

Convinced that Simply Red made good records and that the singer could sing, Kirkham went off to try and get a spot in the band. "I met Andy Dodd at the offices in Didsbury. We went through what music I liked and he played me some music videos and said it all seemed OK but we'd have to wait for Elliot. When he arrived, he looked me up and down and said, 'You'll do if you can play'. That was it... that was the audition."

Kirkham worked alongside fellow brass player Kellett. "The main solo voice in the band after Mick was the trumpet and that was Tim. I did the section stuff and a couple of solos but there wasn't a great deal to do at first and a lot of the time I was left playing tambourine."

Working with Simply Red on *Men And Women* was a new experience for Kirkham who, for all the excitement of being part of the band, understood that he wasn't quite a fully paid-up member of Simply Red. "I was just another session musician really. It was a six-piece band and Janette and me were the add-ons. We started on the same day and it was the band and us two."

Before *Men And Women* came out, Simply Red's contract switched from Elektra and WEA became the repertoire owners, but the records could still be released on the Elektra label and the band would remain on Elektra in the US.

While the basic line-up of Simply Red remained unchanged for the new album Mick was keen to work with a new producer and Sadkin, the man considered by Galpern for *Picture Book*, was Mick's choice to make the record that became the band's second number 2 in the UK and delivered four hit singles including 'Infidelity', the first song he wrote with Lamont Dozier and Cole Porter's classic 'Ev'ry Time We Say Goodbye'.

Sadkin, who died in a motor accident in Nassau a few months after *Men And Women* came out, was one of the 1980s' hottest producers as a result of his work with the Thompson Twins, Foreigner and Duran Duran, but Hole wasn't convinced he was right for Simply Red. "Mick decided he wanted somebody different for the second album but we all felt it was a pity that he changed from Stewart Levine."

Supporting the March 1987 release of the album, Simply Red set off on another round of touring and promotion which lasted for ten solid months and, as the band's leader, Mick was expected to be available for everybody all the time.

"The pressure was always on Mick," explains former Warner executive Anne-Marie Nicol, "because in the media's eyes he was Simply Red. I promoted the band as Simply Red but he was the spokesman, the most articulate and to be honest I don't think the others were that bothered about doing promotion."

The move from almost nobody wanting to know you to everybody clamouring for a piece of you wasn't easy on Mick according to Nicol who travelled the world with him and the band as they plugged their records. "It put huge pressure on Mick who has always had his own insecurities but as he became

Mick dj-ing in New York

more famous he became a much nicer person. He was bolshy and difficult but through the years and because of his success he actually became much nicer."

The focus on Mick as singer, writer and spokesman was something that band member Kirkham understood from day one. "I always thought from the very first day that Simply Red was Mick. He had this idea of how everything should be and his personality always rode over everything else and, as it worked, nobody bothered to take him to task."

"In America Bob Krasnow was flipping over Men And Women. *He was convinced it was much better than* Picture Book, *he was obsessed about it and apparently threw loads and loads of money at it but it didn't stick. I thought it didn't stick because the album didn't sound very good. We did do a lot of promotion in America and we didn't get much back and that was difficult for us."*

Despite the odd differences of opinion, the partnership of Rashman and Dodd was also proving effective, efficient and ultimately successful in taking Mick and Simply Red up the ladder of success, and their efforts were appreciated by those who had to deal with them on a daily basis.

"Elliot was creatively the manager – he and Mick were joined at the hip," says Hole. "Andy was more the logistics man and dealt with the money. You talked to Andy about the deal and he was pragmatic and calm and a pleasure to deal with." According to Hole, Elliot was, however, a completely different sort of animal. "He was irrational, fiery, up and down and thought the world was against him. He and Mick were so close, very, very tight and on a mission together."

Dodd's own analysis of how things were structured within the new Simply Red management operation was pretty much in line with the outside world's view. "I think it's absolutely right to say that Elliot had greater involvement with the creative aspects while I was more involved in the business side of things, but neither role was exclusive."

In fact Rashman and Dodd discussed with each other all the issues regarding Mick and his band and, according to Dodd, it was a full-time job. "We lived in the same place for four years from 1985 and there was no escaping the business of the business. I remember sleeping and working in the same room for the first 18 months – it was insane really." Dealing with the demands of an international music market meant the two managers started work at 8.30 in the morning and would not stop "until America calmed down at around midnight," is Dodd's recollection of an average day.

From his position within the band it was just as clear to Kirkham how things worked. "The band was absolutely run by Mick, Elliot and Andy – Andy did the business while Mick and Elliot were the creative forces. But I always got the sense that when it came down to it, Mick had the final say on everything to do with the music."

Above: The brass section: Ian Kirkham and Tim Kellett

A further two years down the line after *Men And Women*, Simply Red released their third album *A New Flame* in early 1989 and Levine was brought back into the fold... and Hole was a prime mover. "I was the architect in getting Mick back with Stewart and it wasn't easy. They were both proud people and Stewart was upset that Mick didn't use him on the second album.

"And even though that album wasn't as big a hit as everybody hoped, Mick wasn't the type who would readily admit he'd made a wrong decision. It was a case of massaging them back together."

As they started to work together on the new album, Mick and Levine also agreed on the need to change the band's line-up one more time and Brazilian guitarist Heitor T.P. was recruited to replace Aziz Ibrahim, who had joined after the second album in place of Richardson.

Mick continued his writing collaboration with Motown legend Dozier and worked for the first time with ex-Crusader Joe Sample on songs recorded in the Caribbean island of Montserrat, where Levine had chosen George Martin's AIR Studios as the venue for *A New Flame*.

The end product became Simply Red's first UK number one album and it also delivered four hit singles including a cover version of 'If You Don't Know Me By Now'. While it peaked at number two in the UK, the record brought Mick and Simply Red their second number 1 hit in America, putting them on a par with the likes of John Lennon, David Bowie and Queen as one of just 15 UK acts to notch up two US chart-topping singles.

"I look back now at having had two number ones in America and think it's quite an addition to your CV; it's quite a good club to be in."

'If You Don't Know Me By Now', written by Kenny Gamble and Leon Huff and a 1973 top ten hit for Harold Melvin & The Blue Notes, followed Mick's previous hit cover versions from his two previous albums – The Valentine Brothers' 'Money's Too Tight To Mention' and Porter's 1944 classic 'Ev'ry Time We Say Goodbye'.

"It was reassuring to have a number one with 'If You Don't Know Me By Now' because we were wondering if we had kinda blown it. I was a bit frightened of it because I thought the song had been released too much. But a lot of the time the views didn't just come from me. The band were playing the stuff all the time and they had a view but a lot of the time the record company would just say they wanted to release a track as a single and we'd say, 'Alright' – it was very hard to be against something when they're saying they want to do it. I didn't know whether they were right with 'If You Don't Know Me By Now' but we took a gamble with it."

Mick's knowledge of and enthusiasm for black music made him a hit with America's urban media, while his records continued to be well received at black radio and, according to Barbaris, covering the Harold Melvin classic was never going to be a problem for Mick. "He was so good that it was like, 'hats off to the white boy'."

As the man charged with promoting the songs composed by Mick, Peter Reichardt, then head of EMI Music, had a vested interest in what Mick wrote and recorded but the cover versions were never an issue. "They've never bothered me. It's foolhardy for a publisher to say to an artist you've got to write every song on every album. Mick has very clear-cut ideas on exactly which songs he wants to cover and 99 times out of 100 he's dead right."

Undeterred by Mick's success rate, Reichardt still tried to make a contribution over the years. "I kinda like to put forward a few ideas which I have done via the management but nothing ever comes of it, because he does focus on his own ideas."

Released in February, *A New Flame* became the first album of 1989 to sell a million copies in the UK where it topped the charts for four weeks and, now firmly established in pop music's premier league, Simply Red set off on almost two years of constant globe trotting.

Reichardt in fact first became involved with Mick and Simply Red around the time of *A New Flame* when the SBK music publishing company he worked for was acquired by EMI Music Publishing in 1988. He was already aware of Simply Red through their first two albums but saw the follow-up album to *Picture Book* as a disappointment. "I think it was that thing about the second album always being the difficult one."

With the third album in the can and ready to go, Reichardt began to get more involved. "There was a certain nervousness about the album and I helped out in every area I could and I remember giving them a non-recoupable advance – and no publisher likes to give non-recoupable money – but Elliot squeezed it out of me, and it turned out to be money well spent."

Reichardt is one music executive who believes that the business of recording is best left to the musicians. "It was not my role in life to visit artists in the studio and I never feel comfortable there. The way Mick and Stewart Levine worked was that they would go away, do what ever they did, and hey presto! When the album was delivered we all thought it was real good, it certainly sounded good and Stewart had done his job. The album put Mick right back at the top."

The team of Rashman and Dodd was also now established as a major force in the music business and Spinoza watched from the sidelines as Simply Red and So What Arts took on the world. "The Elliot and Andy dynamic was interesting. They had – including Mick – a Manchester/Liverpool edge about them, even in Andy's calmer style. They took an anti-establishment attitude about not doing things like everyone else."

Gold Awards for *A New Flame,* Clockwise:
Heitor TP, Ian Kirkham, Chris Joyce,
Tony Bowers, Fritz McIntyre, Mick,
Elliot Rashman and Tim Kellett

Mick and Fritz McIntyre in US record store

"We were perceived as being outspoken and Elliot especially so," agrees Dodd, adding, "the good cop, bad cop routine was fairly accurate."

Elliot's fixation on Mick and Simply Red was there for all to see and while the band were enjoying their US number one single, the album's performance in America – where it peaked at 22 – was a major source of concern to the management and the UK record company, according to Hole.

"*A New Flame* went really well everywhere in the world except the US. There had been a big falling-out with Krasnow at a playback for the album in Los Angeles when he made some undiplomatic comments about the album not fitting America's radio format. The band and everybody were distraught and Elliot, who was never a great diplomat, had a major clash with Krasnow who then got angry with me because I still thought it was a great record."

If Rashman was the 'bad cop' who complained the loudest, his partner was no less disappointed with results in America. "The American record-buying public has absolutely no loyalty and irrespective of how many number ones you have, you still have to be in their face, constantly reminding them that you're still at it," is Dodd's reading of the situation.

"Unfortunately they always seem to want reminding at seven in the morning – drive time – and that was never going to happen with Mick. Also it was crazy to ignore our extremely successful core market in Europe to chase the mythical American Dream. Nine times out of ten it never happens. However, I would say that we invested far more in America than we ever got back."

The lack of success in America, together with the comments made by the head of their US label, drove the So What team towards the office of Bob Morgado, the head of the Warner Music Group. "*A New Flame* had been such a big international hit that Krasnow was caught out," explains Hole, "and Elliot and Andy used their power to get Morgado to switch the band from Elektra to East West, which we had begun using in the UK and was then launched in the US."

Levine, however, is not convinced that it was simply a case of the records not fitting America's style of formatted radio. "I think things went beyond that. I thought right from the beginning that Mick never spent the kind of time in America that was necessary for a British band to create a real audience. He had number one records, so he should have been off and running."

Simply Red's refusal to play the heartland of America, according to Levine, was more relevant than radio's reluctance to schedule their records. "There was this perception that this band didn't take their hats off to America, never embraced America and that they had a bit of a snooty attitude. It was a combination of many things, but he didn't work really hard in America."

Levine's view is shared in part by Dodd who acknowledges that in order to achieve success in America artists need to live there for nine months to a year

Mick and Elliot Rashman, 1986

and "spend sixteen hours a day kissing ass." He acknowledges that this wasn't his act's style. "Mick didn't tell them he loved them enough and didn't reassure America that he wasn't going away – and he was a self-confessed socialist to boot."

One man who was impressed with *A New Flame* – and the title track in particular – was Mick's dad, who reckons it's his favourite song from the enormous catalogue of songs his son has recorded over two decades. "*A New Flame* is my favourite track. I particularly like the video with him dancing with the girl with the turban on who was just like Carmen Miranda. It was probably about a girlfriend but I don't know which one."

Videos were in fact becoming an increasingly important part of marketing Simply Red around the world. Unable to be in Australia, America, Italy and England all at the same time, videos were often the only tool a record company had to help in the promotion of a record.

"Singles were always important in Australia," says Ikin, "and because Simply Red couldn't visit Australia for promotion we were dependent on videos. Australia was one of the first markets where TV shows were built around videos so these were important shows for Simply Red who always delivered good videos, and that was important in a market which you can't visit very often."

Dealing with the fame and adulation was something, according to Harding, that Mick grew into, albeit gradually. "The first success – going from being on the dole to a big star – took some adjusting to as, at the time, he was pretty gobby and some people really never forgave him, even though he learned how to play the game."

After the global success of *A New Flame*, Mick, as always, returned to Manchester and a life that, at bordered on the normal in some ways. "He came in the office one day and wanted to get some new phones for his house from the BT shop in Manchester's Arndale Centre," recalls Harding who got the job of accompanying the star on the shopping trip.

"By the time we got to the Centre there were thousands of people turning and looking at him and I thought, 'How do you deal with this?' but he was fine, smiling at everybody and signing autographs. So he did learn how to handle it."

By the end of 1989 *A New Flame* had sold over six million copies worldwide and, after a swift three-month 30-date tour of Europe early in 1990, Mick settled down to begin work on the next album which would eventually see the light of day in late 1991.

For the people at WEA UK Simply Red's international success came as a welcome bonus alongside the company's well-established roster of US artists,

according to Moira Bellas. "The only other global act we had was the Pretenders. It was good to have a new band that achieved global success and Mick and Simply Red certainly worked hard to get there."

At the same time as preparing the album, Mick was also exploring other music that was making the headlines and the airwaves and, as always, was thinking how he could improve his band and their sound.

He became aware of a Japanese programmer called Gota from Soul II Soul's debut album *Club Classics Vol. One*, where he shared the credits with Jazzie B and Nellee Hooper, and Mick decided that he could bring something new to Simply Red.

While he was aware of the band, Gota was not too sure who or what Simply Red actually were. "In Japan I had a 12'' version of 'Love Fire' and was deeply in love with dub reggae and at first I thought Simply Red was a reggae band. Then I recognised the voice from having heard 'Holding Back The Years'."

Fresh from Soul II Soul, Gota moved over to begin work with Mick on the new album. "He just said, 'Give me whatever you feel, give me your thoughts' and neither he nor Stewart gave me any particular instructions; it was just about my programming and groove ideas."

As the album progressed, Gota began to spend time with drummer Joyce. They talked about drum rhythms on the various new tracks but he had only one thing on his mind: "I was only there as the programmer, not the drummer."

However, it became obvious that Gota was also an extraordinary percussionist and pretty soon he became a permanent member of the band and Joyce, an original member and veteran of three albums, was out. Original bassist Bowers – a member with Joyce of early 80s band Durutti Column – had left previously, to be replaced by Shaun Ward.

Back in Manchester, Spinoza reflected on the changing line-up of Simply Red. "I don't think Mick had a master plan before *Picture Book* but after that, with advice from Stewart Levine and the record company, he realised changes had to be made to the band and they were made whenever it became necessary."

While he always knew how Simply Red worked, he had it confirmed to him by manager Rashman. "Elliot always spun the line that Simply Red was a solo artist with various musicians; it was Mick and his backing band. That was always going to be the case, no matter what people thought."

For Rashman the sacking of Joyce – one of his oldest friends and a man he had brought to the party – was, according to Spinoza, not easy. "Elliot told me that sacking Chris was the hardest thing he ever had to do."

Top: Gota, Mick and Tim Kellett at
Gota's wedding

Bottom: Recording *Stars* at
Condulmer Studio, Venice

Mick's father, however, was not surprised by the changes that were made. "He has always been a perfectionist when it came to his music, and he does have a bit of a ruthless streak when it comes to getting the band right and letting people go if they weren't right," says Reg.

"Changes in the band are almost exclusively because you think the music can be improved. It's almost always about a musical situation. But if we are going to look for reference points on how we handled these kind of things, I would ask people to look more into the world of soul and reggae and blues and jazz than in this kind of, 'Well the four of us are married and we're always going to be in the same band for the rest of our lives'. That really isn't what my culture is all about. Most of my culture is about the Stax and Motown bands, where one or two musicians regularly changed and you ended up with a rotating family of working musicians."

From his position inside the band, Kirkham also had a first-hand view of what was going on and his concern was how it would affect the sound of Simply Red. "There was a certain sound that now defines some of the earlier Simply Red songs," is his assessment. "After Tony and Chris left it was hard to go back to some of the earlier songs and get something that sounds that distinctive. It was not a natural way to play but, what made those songs sound like they do, was the strange style they used to play."

Firmly ensconced in the So What Arts operation, Harding was on the verge of becoming project manager of the next album when the changes were made, and it didn't make for a fun time at the office. "The band changes were a bit brutal and I was in the office when certain phone calls were made and it wasn't really very pleasant."

As the record executive in closest contact with Simply Red and So What, Max Hole was able to share his own views on the band's musical prowess with the powers that be. "There was an overall feeling that the rhythm section wasn't very strong and I think we sort of contributed to the changes, but it was mainly Mick and Elliot who made the decisions. Even so, I was still shocked when Chris Joyce got fired."

"Not every departure from Simply Red has been acrimonious. It's like a break up with a girlfriend, sometimes you mutually agree to a change. It's not such a big deal with a free-flowing band, they chop and change all the time and it's perfectly acceptable."

Despite what Rashman told Spinoza and others, Harding wasn't so sure that everybody understood how Simply Red worked. "I think Simply Red was always Mick but things like, 'This is Mick Hucknall's band, Mick's the leader of the band,' were never said explicitly, so some band members may have deluded themselves about their role in Simply Red."

That said, Harding firmly believes that the rhythm section being assembled for the new album was much more accomplished. "Finding someone like Gota was

definitely a step forward for the band, but I do know that Mick was genuinely fond of Chris and felt bad about having to drop him."

"People come and go, it's a fluid thing, but Simply Red is one person" is how Peter Reichardt assesses the situation. "Mick knows that as a brand Simply Red is important, but you're never sure what Simply Red is going to be. Bringing in new musicians worked because Stewart knew players from different musical backgrounds."

Assigned to the new East West division of Warner Music UK, led by Max Hole, the new Simply Red began working on the album that the world would come to know as *Stars* in a studio in Paris where, project manager Harding recalls, things were far from satisfactory.

"We started recording in Paris just a couple of days after the Gulf War broke out and, when we arrived, we found that the hotel was opposite the offices of Iraq and Kuwait airways. Then we got to the studio which was outside the city and it felt like being in a bunker; we had the television on and there were these films of the Gulf War. It was all very depressing and the facilities weren't right either."

Charged with changing things, Levine quickly came up with a studio in Venice which suited Italy-loving Mick and gave Gota a chance to mix with his new soul mates. "Being isolated with all the musicians in Paris and then Venice was good for me, and when we had drinks and dinner all together it was great fun."

While it may have been just fun for Gota, it turned out to be a revelation for Mick. "One night after dinner when maybe I was a bit drunk," explains Gota, "we were back at the villa and I started playing on this drum kit. It was first time I had played drums during the sessions as I was programming and everybody just turned and said, 'I didn't know you could drum.'" At that point Gota became Simply Red's new drummer.

Although he wasn't closely involved in the recording of *Stars*, Hole flew out to Venice, while Mick and Levine were still mixing the new album, to hear how things were progressing. "The first thing you do in those circumstances is listen and think, 'What's the single?' I thought I heard at least two. 'Something Got Me Started' was an obvious first choice and I thought 'Stars' sounded like a really good second single."

Confident with what he had heard of the new album, Hole met up with Sylvia Rhone, the head of East West Records in America – Simply Red's new home in the US – but she wasn't quite so sure. "She was worried about the records and radio formatting in the US and in a way she was right, because it was a difficult radio record for America."

Working on what was to be her last Simply Red record as an employee of East West, Barbaris – who had returned from Geffen Records to become head of

publicity for the label – recalls a different set of circumstances. "'Something Got Me Started' was doing well and the truth was that it was competing for airplay with En Vogue (also signed to East West) who we were also working at the time," she explains. "But because of the lack of commitment from the management for Simply Red to work America, a decision was taken within the label to chase the En Vogue record and we kind of killed the Simply Red record.

"We could have done more on the label side but it was sort of mutually resistant. They didn't think Sylvia Rhone and her people were doing their job and she didn't think Simply Red were doing their job to help her," says Barbaris. "So everybody kind of packed it in."

Adopting a realistic attitude towards the performance of *Stars* in the US, co-manager Dodd admits it wasn't a record that was ever going to appeal to the record buyers of America. "In Sylvia's mind, she couldn't hear it on the American radio formats and the timing didn't fall well as *Stars* coincided with the mainstream emergence of hip hop in America – that was what we were up against. America just heard a European record and decided to spend their money elsewhere."

While *Stars* sold around 700,000 in America – "with just a couple of TV performances and around four shows" – Barbaris doesn't agree that American radio formats were the problem. "The records were fine for America and still are, there's no problem there. The records could have done better and East West could have done a better job, but the UK could have done a better job and given us more access to the band."

The fact that the album peaked at number 79 in America, while the highest-placed single from *Stars* in the US was 'Something Got Me Started' at 23, certainly shocked Kirkham. "The thought was that other albums had done fine in America, so why wouldn't *Stars* do well? It had more accessible songs on it and I just can't see why America didn't get it although maybe it was just all down to the radio they have over there."

Stars might have been hard work for America but around the rest of the world it was a sensational bestseller. In the UK it was the top selling album for two successive years, by which time it had sold over eight million copies worldwide.

With five hit singles, *Stars* took Simply Red back to number one in the UK – on five separate occasions and for a total of 12 weeks – where the album topped the 2 million sales mark.

"The sales figures for Stars *reflect what happened in the UK because in some other territories* A New Flame *has turned out to have done better. It was one of those* Sergeant Pepper *moments in a way – where something gets a moment in time and just hits home. You have to make that kind of comparison if you've had the biggest album for two years in a row. That's a big album...* Brothers In Arms,

Zanna

Zanna

that kind of thing. It was in the top five biggest selling British albums of all time but was really only a British phenomenon, but still I was quite satisfied with thinking, 'Well, I've done it'."

Taking delivery of the new album, Hole could only hope that *Stars* would do "as well as *A New Flame*" and continue his new working relationship with Mick and his managers. "It takes a long time to get into their circle, and once you get in and they trust you, then you can get things done. But things were made difficult by the fact that there was friction with some of the people at the US label who weren't quite in the circle."

In fact, promoting, marketing and ultimately selling *Stars* was relatively painless for Hole and his crew. "When it works, it all seems easy. The making of the record was easy, Mick and Stewart were getting on well, the band had a good rhythm section and the creative side of it was easy. It was a great team and it seemed we could no wrong."

East West started the ball rolling with a video for 'Something Got Me Started' and followed it with a clip for 'Stars' which involved a designer/ stylist/ photographer overseeing the art direction for the album some seven years after she first saw the band on stage.

After her experience at the Hammersmith Odeon in 1985, Zanna had established herself as an important creative force in the entertainment industry but it was a photograph appearing in the London *Evening Standard* which opened the door into the world of Simply Red.

"Elliot had seen the picture and called me to an interview with Mick. I thought long and hard about what to wear to meet Mr. Hucknall," she recalls. Opting for a man's suit and tie – "It was important as a woman photographer to remove the woman part" – she thinks she made the right impression. "I think Mick was quite shocked by the Charlie Chaplin look, and always had a strange opinion about me ever after."

Zanna's first task was to shoot a set of shots for press use and she was warned in advance about what to expect. "Elliot told me that Mick didn't like having his photograph taken so he might just walk out after 15 minutes. Then he built up this whole anxiety thing about how I was working with a big artist so early on in my career and needed to do a good job."

In the end, Mick stayed the course and Zanna's shots for the sleeve of the single 'Something Got Me Started' served as the inspiration for the supporting video which, to her surprise, she did not direct. "I was a little bit miffed that the video was so reminiscent of my photo session but when we were shooting the *Stars* album cover Elliot asked me if I would like to direct the video for the 'Stars' track."

Although she had never directed a video before, Zanna knew how it worked and set off with the track to the Edinburgh Film Festival to seek inspiration. "I saw

lots of films but one that influenced me a lot was called *Europa*. It was a film with collages of images where sometimes things were very big – big clocks and big trains – in relation to the people."

Armed with her idea, she described what she had in mind to the East West people who, fired up by her enthusiasm, gave her a producer to work with. She produced a treatment and storyboard which, in her words, "outlined the surreal Dali-esque nature combined with some sort of sexuality."

With a desert as a necessary prop for the video, Zanna worked out the logistics of using the Sahara. "It involved a 14-hour journey for Mick, who was very busy at the time, and the idea of him travelling to the desert to shoot in sand dunes within the time frame was impossible."

Zanna's Plan B involved finding more accessible sand dunes and more research led her to the Californian town of Baker. "It's between LA and Las Vegas," recalls the London-based photographer, "and has two diners, two motels and the tallest thermometer in the world – and oddly, it was going to be easier for Mick to get there than to Morocco."

The giant stars used in the 'Stars' video were made in London (by the company that made Pink Floyd's famous pig for their *Animals* album cover) and shipped to America while the location manager went out to shoot some footage of the dunes. He came back with the film and some bad news for Zanna.

"He said the dunes were unused for most of the year but the two days we wanted were booked for a dune buggy rally with 20,000 Hells Angles riding about leaving tyre tracks all over the sand. Then when I drove out I found a *Vogue* photo shoot going on at the same time."

With her chosen dunes overrun with bikers and models, Zanna was forced to go further into the desert to find more sand and then, when Mick finally arrived to shoot the video, the California sun disappeared. With the film in the can, Zanna and the crew returned to England to see what they'd got.

"We looked at the rushes and there was a problem with the quality and I was just about ready to commit suicide. But it turned out to be a problem with the tele-cine house and not the film so that was OK, but I look at the video now and I absolutely hate it.

"At the time it was exciting, even when we had to put in a fake sunny sky. In fact it was nominated for a BRIT Award and, at the end of the day, everybody was happy."

With a new album and two videos in the can, Hole and his East West team were more than just happy. "The first video was perfect and the 'Stars' video was great and it just seemed we could do no wrong," he explains, and it seems that Mick was just as satisfied.

"He called up a lot to find out how things were going with *Stars* and he was thrilled because he set out to write the whole album himself as he didn't want anyone doubting his ability as a writer."

It wasn't just in the UK that *Stars* was making an impact. Platinum sales awards poured in from around the world and Warner Music International's Nicol was excited from the first moment she heard it. "It was a great album and the 'Something Got Me Started' re-mix put him into a different audience bracket abroad. It moved him into a whole new segment of the market, and was played in the hippest clubs all over the place.

"It all came together with that album. It was a culmination of the previous three albums and the learning process that Mick had gone through to get to that specific place," she says.

One person who missed out on the *Stars* story was record executive Bellas who went with WEA UK when Simply Red moved over to East West. "I always believed Mick would be hugely successful and it was a disappointment not to be working with them when they achieved their extraordinary success with *Stars*."

In the final months of 1992, a new face appeared in the East West team when Ian Grenfell joined as head of international. His first job was to try and put some spark into one of the few territories that had underperformed with *Stars*.

"In fact, my very first day was spent in Tokyo presenting the album to a new Warner affiliate in Japan. The plan was to get them to re-release *Stars* in Japan as the album came round for its second Christmas. At the end of the day, we managed to get the sales up from 40,000 to just over 70,000."

In fact, the release of *Stars* was the first album under a new deal Simply Red had signed with EMI Music Publishing, which Reichardt recalls as being a tough piece of business. "The negotiations were protracted and Elliot, being Elliot, was pretty hard on the deal, but that was fine."

The record was also the first album comprised of songs written or co-written by Mick, and Reichardt had a great sense of relief that the deal had been signed. "Nobody could have foreseen what *Stars* was going to achieve, it took on a life if its own. The pressures on Mick to promote it month after month were immense but, in strictly business terms, I did thank God we got the deal done."

For new boy Grenfell the next step was actually meeting Mick and his management team, and that happened in the lounge at Heathrow Airport in early 1993 on the way to South Africa for a television talk show. "I remember him just staring at me blankly and obviously wondering who the hell I was," he recalls.

"Then when we got there I found myself with these two mad Mancunians and one mad scouser – Andy Dodd – who just talked and shouted at each other non-stop while nobody listened to anything. I just got on the phone to get details of the England versus San Marino football match, which I thought might be a useful thing to do."

For Hole, who was famous for telling anyone who would listen that Mick could sing a half-decent song and turn it into a hit, the global success of *Stars* proved everything he had always thought about the Mancunian singer. "Number one, he's a fantastic singer and he's proved himself to be a good writer. He's also very determined, very ambitious and hard-working. But he isn't always easy and he doesn't always have a lot of charm but he could always turn it on. He went on the *Parkinson* programme to sing 'Stars' and was so charming and funny in the interview that the record just erupted after that."

"It was all very strange; like music beyond your control where it goes into the twilight zone and where everyone and his granny has to have that album as part of their coffee table set. I do think it is the best album I've made so far but my biggest memory of Stars *is Max Hole telling me that we spent less money on marketing* Stars *than we did on* A New Flame, *yet at one point he couldn't get the CDs made quickly enough."*

Dealing with the difficult, and sometimes not so charming, tough guy was all in a day's work for Hole, who could always turn to manager Rashman when the going got really hard. "We used to play this game between us of who was going to tell Mick the bad news about something. We'd say, 'OK, I'll soften him up and then you tell him,' or the other way round. Between us we had a good way of persuading him to do things."

The success of *Stars* set new records in the UK and the total sales figure of four million is a figure which Grenfell, with the advent of digital technology and downloads, believes may never be reached again in this country by any album.

The four year gap between *Stars* and the follow-up album *Life* was the longest period without an album so far for Simply Red, although a live EP from the world-famous Montreux Jazz Festival peaked at number 11 in 1992.

"The Montreux EP was a great piece of strategy and a great piece of marketing and it showed that there was a jazz side to our music. I've held a torch for jazz throughout my career and I know it's a minority thing but if you do have an inflection of it in the music, I think it lends sophistication to it. It makes me proud of the music I make as opposed to just making pop hits; I want that little bit of sophistication otherwise I don't feel satisfied."

Simply Red filled the time by touring almost non-stop in 1992, playing over 120 shows around the world followed by just a dozen in 1993 in Latin America and the UK. With no concerts in 1994, as *Stars* celebrated 134 weeks in the UK album chart, the creative process required to produce a new album was well underway.

Life arrived without long-time horn player Kellet and bass player Ward but included reggae stars Sly Dunbar, Robbie Shakespeare and Bootsy Collins.

The new album arrived on the scene as not only the band's third successive chart-topper, but also their third album in a row to enter the chart at number one.

"It was always intentional to have a two-year gap between albums. It was something Elliot and I formulated and I remember being obsessive about that kind of gap because I thought it was good to go away. 'How can I miss you when you won't go away?' was a phrase we used all the time. But Elliot felt we took too long to make Life *– he said four years was too long."*

During a *Life* tour that stretched over nine months during 1995 and 1996, bassist Steve Lewinson and vocalist Sarah Brown made their debuts with the band, who notched up their first ever UK number one hit single with 'Fairground' and followed up with four more hits.

Even though Mick and Levine were now credited as co-producers, it was clear to those closest to the band that the making of *Life* had its problems. Harding took the view that Mick had served his apprenticeship as a producer and was now ready to go it alone. "He had learned how to produce from Stewart and didn't want him involved except to oversee things, which didn't please Stewart very much," explains Harding, who adds that one day in the midst of all this Levine explained his definition of a producer. "He said it was simple… 'Artists come to me with songs and I turn 'em into records.'"

For Hole, following the UK's biggest selling album for two successive years was another problem. "We weren't really involved in the making of the record – it was Mick and Stewart as usual – but when they had finished, Elliot and I were worried that we didn't have a first single."

"We thought we had a pretty good album but no first single, and we sort of worked outside Mick. I got Mark Stent to remix three or four songs including 'Fairground'. I think the deal I told Mick was that I would pay for the four mixes and, if he didn't like them, I wouldn't charge him, but if he used them then they would become a recording cost."

With Rashman behind him all the way, the remixed 'Fairground' became the front-runner as first single from the new album but, according to Hole, Mick wasn't convinced. "I gave him the mixes and he didn't like them at all. He said he was going to remix, and maybe with Stewart he did go away and remix 'Fairground', but it was then that we all decided that 'Fairground' should be the single."

When Grenfell first heard the new album he too had reservations about some of the music, although everything else seemed to be perfect. "It was the best set-up record I'd ever been involved with. The campaign dreamed up by Elliot and Zanna was going to be bigger and better than anything before but with hindsight it was probably too corporate. Because it was following *Stars* people thought that was what it had to be – big and expensive."

Zanna

However, Grenfell's reservations about the music were put to one side when he was played a remix of 'Fairground'. "You always need a track that's going to be played on radio and when I heard 'Fairground' I instantly got the shiver up the spine and knew it was a huge single."

But, not everybody agreed. "Brazil said they didn't like 'Fairground' because it had Brazilians in it and sounded Latin. They said, 'We do this music, we want Simply Red to be international not local' and Germany's sales manager thought the imaging was all too cold," Grenfell explains. "He was possibly right but the imaging was strong and the TV advert was so powerful that I thought it was worth another half-a-million records."

In fact the TV commercial – featuring Mick jogging and walking on a running machine – very nearly didn't happen at all as the singer had had a hernia operation just three days before the shoot, and was still suffering the after-effects of surgery as he climbed on the treadmill.

Life was issued by East West with an expensive launch and great expectations. "We were issuing the follow-up to a blockbuster. We spent lots of money on a massive launch and trumpeted the album all over the world," recalls Hole. "'Fairground' was at number one for four weeks, the album went straight in at number one and it was all great but then it didn't perform after that. Stars hadn't done well in America and this one did even less well, and my impression was that it was all about their radio formatting again."

"After Stars they set up the Life album to be as big as Stars, and in fact they spent more money on the marketing. It was all so polished and I just felt that I was going along on a treadmill and yet everybody was making out that I was making all the decisions. But I don't think I was. I think I was in a kind of proletariat set-up and I started to get very lost. I began thinking, 'I don't like this, I don't trust this' – it was all too polished, too manufactured. But I went along with it because the whole kind of momentum that was behind Stars was naturally leading there. My management were saying that we didn't want to make the mistake of making it as big as Stars but we were doing just that and it did become a bit of a treadmill. And I was as guilty as everyone else for not getting a grip, coming back down to earth and just enjoying the music.

I always respected Bruce Springsteen for seeing that he made a massive album and then the next album was like an acoustic album. That was appealing to me."

The problems with America and Simply Red were not going to go away easily, and after the disappointment of Stars the relationship between Mick, his managers and Sylvia Rhone got even more difficult, according to Grenfell.

"Elliot and Andy had been asked by Warner to draw up a plan of what they thought it would take to break Simply Red in America. This was sort of forced on Sylvia who was told to follow a marketing plan that she really didn't want… it all got very uncomfortable," adds Grenfell, who understood that America wanted Simply Red to be an R&B band.

"Stars was probably the 'whitest' album the band had made but it captured a wave in Europe, which was feeling less American at that time. And as soon as I heard 'Fairground' I thought that it was going to work everywhere but in America because it was so non-R&B."

The release of Life in 1995 marked the arrival within the Simply Red management team of their former publicist Lisa Barbaris who had switched from East West to create the So What Arts America arm of the operation. But she was only able to make the jump through the generosity of Simply Red.

"I was unhappy at East West and Mick, Andy and Elliot knew it. Then Andy called me to say I should quit my job as they were going to give me a loan and fund me to start my own PR company and also to manage Simply Red in America," she explains, while at the same time recalling that one of her first management tasks still ranks as her worst Simply Red moment.

Courtesy of East West, the band were offered a spot performing at Ted Turner's Goodwill Games initiative in New York's Battery Park. "The label made all sorts of promises to me and Elliot," recounts Barbaris, "but when it came to it nobody was there because it wasn't promoted properly, and no one even came from the label because they weren't interested either."

On top of that, Barbaris had to get Mick up at the crack of dawn next day – "and we know how much he likes doing that" – for a live morning television show, and when they didn't get round to interviewing Mick, the fledgling manager went to work. "I forced the show to tape an interview that they could show later and then we got in the limo to go to the airport to fly off to LA. In the car Mick said to me, 'I think it's best if we sit apart on the plane.' He was upset and he could have fired me because everything that could have gone wrong went wrong. I was a young manager and part of it was my fault for trusting people to do things they said they'd do… and he trusted me and I let him down."

Barbaris puts her survival down to a combination of her own ability, her long standing friendship with Mick and, perhaps, her sex. "I'm a girl, and Mick's always nicer to girls. When Elliot couldn't get Mick to do things he'd call me and ask me to try and talk him into it."

Midway through the 1996 concert dates, Mick's combined enthusiasm for Manchester, football and Old Trafford saw the band return from the European leg of the tour to fit in an important one-off show. Two days after playing Ancona in Italy and four days before returning to Athens, Mick led the band out at Old Trafford on June 29 for a special concert celebrating the Euro '96 soccer tournament.

A week earlier 'We're In This Together' – the official song for the Euro '96 European football championships, written by Mick and recorded by Simply Red – entered the British charts and it also heralded a significant new look for the long-haired singer.

Pele, Mick and Bobby Charlton, Euro '96

Designer and photographer Zanna was working with Mick at the time of 'We're In This Together' when the question of his trademark dreadlocks came into the conversation. "He asked me about cutting them off. He was struggling enormously with the weight of his hair, which was damaging the roots. So we cut them off to give him this whole new look, which I thought was great."

Within a year of the release of *Life*, the talk was about a possible greatest hits collection from Simply Red which, for their record company, was an urgent need. "*Life* did OK but obviously not as well as *Stars*," recalls Hole, "and the hits album was all about money. We were having a bad year at Warner and the people at the top wanted a Simply Red hits collection, and I was put under a lot of pressure to deliver one for the good and glory of the corporation."

At a private lunch between Mick and Hole at Mick's house, the East West exec chose to raise the subject of a Hits collection. "Mick was preparing pasta and as we chatted I sort of mentioned that I thought he should do a greatest hits album. Mick, as was usually the case when you said something he didn't want to hear, just said, 'No way, I'm not doing it.'"

"I didn't want to release the Greatest Hits *album. I wasn't happy about it as I thought it was too premature. It was a time when I was falling apart from Elliot and it represented an idea that I had done my best work or come to an end while in actual fact I was in it for the long haul. But we had enough hits to do it and I went along with it.*

I liked the cover picture very much and specifically insisted on Greatest Hits *because if I wanted it to be a Best Of it would have been mostly album tracks and not hit singles."*

Knowing full well that to argue further would lead to a major falling-out, Hole tucked into his lunch and changed the subject, comforted by the fact that he had the support of Mick's management. "Elliot and Andy were both in favour because they knew it was a good idea strategically and worth a lot of money."

Hole's next tack was to offer a multi-million deal in order to get the *Greatest Hits* album and re-negotiate Simply Red's recording deal at the same time. And – surprise, surprise – it worked.

"Word came back that we could have the *Hits*," says Hole, but that wasn't the end of it. "Then we had an argument about 'Ev'ry Time We Say Goodbye' which Mick did not want on the album. I told him that if I bought a Simply Red Hits collection and it wasn't on there I'd be disappointed. He was adamant and we were so desperate for the album that we just said, 'Sod it.'"

If the Cole Porter classic wasn't going to be included on the album, a brand new track boasting a major US hit-making trio was especially recorded for the collection. 'Angel' featured the combined talents of Fugees Wyclef Jean, Pras Michel and Lauryn Hill and romped to number four in the charts while the *Greatest Hits* collection made it four number one albums in a row for Simply Red.

Top: With members of Germany's
Euro '96 squad

Right: Performing at Old Trafford,
Manchester, 1996

Bottom: Mick and Sir Alex Ferguson

Simply Red Greatest Hits

"'Angel' was great. They said they wanted an extra track that was original and I always wanted to do the song because I think it's brilliant. I like the Fugees and Sylvia Rhone at East West said she could put it together. I love Lauryn Hill's voice and Wyclef has a lot of talent in production. We did it between other things. I did a bit over here, sent it to them; they did a bit and sent it back and I sang it. Then I did my mix of it and they did their mix of it... that's how we got there."

In the period after *Life* and ahead of the follow-up album *Blue*, Grenfell spotted the first cracks appearing in the Simply Red camp. "The success of 'Fairground' and *Life* masked a lot of problems. Behind the success there was what was going on between Mick and Stewart Levine, and to my mind Mick seemed permanently pissed off during the whole campaign."

The recording and release of *Blue* also saw wholesale changes in the Simply Red camp with original keyboard player, vocalist and composer McIntyre leaving and guitarist Heitor TP also moving on.

For remaining band member Kirkham, the departure of McIntyre, co-writer of hits such as 'Something Got Me Started' and 'Thrill Me', was no real surprise. "I always understood why Tony and Chris went, and Mick and Fritz had this strange relationship where they got on but they didn't. You could never tell which way it was going to be and all the touring wasn't doing Fritz any favours. I think he needed a break from it all."

The 1995 release of *Life* came on the back of Dodd's first decade as co-manager of Simply Red and during those ten years three band members had made a lasting impression – and two of them were about to leave. "The real axis of the band was Mick and Fritz and that continued through to *Life*. The essential sound of Simply Red was Fritz's luxurious keyboard pads supporting Mick's voice and there was a certain tension between them that seemed to work."

Confirming his view that McIntyre was "the bedrock of the band", Dodd, however, saves his highest praise for guitarist Heitor. "He was the most complete musician I have ever come across. Guitar was his first love – and negotiating his fee was his second," says the man who also cannot imagine Simply Red without the multi-talented Kirkham. "He's the only one who can remember all the arrangements."

Meanwhile, for Gota, McIntyre's leaving had another impact. "A lot of Simply Red was Fritz's piano alongside Mick's voice and when Fritz left things had to change." One of those changes was Gota re-joining the fold, but this time as producer with his partner Andy Wright and alongside Mick in a team credited as AGM.

Recorded in London, Jamaica and New York, *Blue* featured over 20 musicians and singers plus the Pro Arte Orchestra with Wright and Gota programming. It also signalled the end of Hole's relationship with Simply Red as he moved on to another record company two months before the album's release.

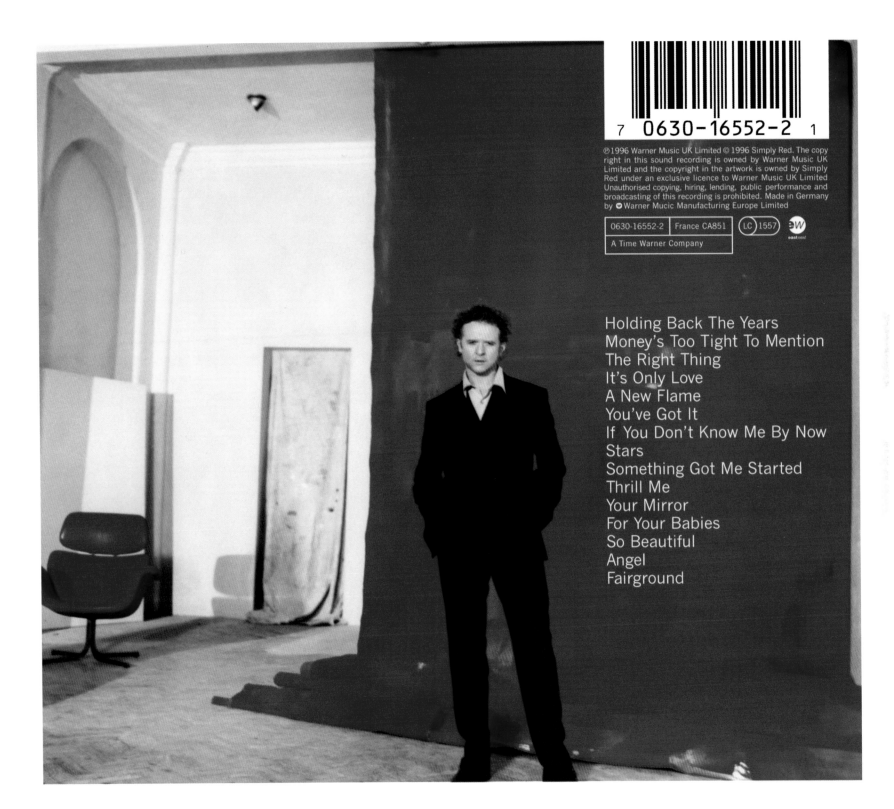

Holding Back The Years
Money's Too Tight To Mention
The Right Thing
It's Only Love
A New Flame
You've Got It
If You Don't Know Me By Now
Stars
Something Got Me Started
Thrill Me
Your Mirror
For Your Babies
So Beautiful
Angel
Fairground

In the period before he left, Hole had been played some of the tracks planned for the new album and had concerns about what he was hearing. "I was hearing stuff I didn't think was very good. The album was being made without Stewart and I thought what was being delivered was weak."

Although he was keen not to go out on a low note, Hole made his feelings known to Simply Red's main man. "Mick was really pissed off at me and we were falling out because I wasn't telling him that everything was great, and for the first time I heard that he had sort of moaned about me to some people at the top at Warners."

With his East West label not having the best of times in the late 1990s, and Mick's relationship with the company almost at breaking point, Hole saw himself as fair game for some sniping but consoled himself with his imminent departure. "I remember thinking that I was leaving at a good time."

Despite Hole's reservations, *Blue* went on to become Simply Red's fifth successive number one album and delivered four top twenty singles – 'Night Nurse', 'Say You Love Me', 'The Air That I Breathe' and 'Ghetto Girl' – of which only the number 7 hit 'Say You Love Me' was written by Mick.

Even though she was art director for the *Stars*, *Life* and *Blue* album covers, Zanna wasn't responsible for the fact that all three covers – and the earlier *Men And Women* cover – ended up being blue. "I think it was Elliot's belief that the colour blue sold better. It was a always a very Renaissance blue, and it was something that Elliot and Mick decided."

Following the band's only three dates in the whole of 1998 at London's Lyceum, Simply Red went back on the road in the middle of the following year as they prepared what would turn out to be their last official album for East West.

In support of their seventh studio album in 15 years, the band travelled from South Africa, through Europe, on to Latin America and back to the UK. They joined in the celebrations for the new millennium at the National Maritime Museum in Greenwich and concluded the tour at Manchester's MEN Arena in May 2000.

Yet, even as the band prepared to start work on the new album, there was still a sense of dismay inside the camp in the wake of the surprise departure of Mick's long-time manager and confidant Elliot Rashman.

Even though he was working with a rival company and no longer in close contact, Hole was still not prepared for the departure of the man who he considered "the most important person besides Mick in the Simply Red story." Mick's dad too was full of praise for the man who guided his son's career. "Elliot was a good manager for Mick, and he owes a lot to Elliot."

Filming the video for 'Your Eyes'

Partner Dodd goes further, declaring that "Simply Red would not have existed without Elliot's vision."

Hole says simply: "It was such a shock when they parted. Throughout the golden era of Simply Red there was a triumvirate of people who dealt with the records – Elliot, Stewart and me. We talked all the time, conspired all the time, decided who would do what to persuade Mick that he ought be doing this or that. It was extraordinary that he left."

"Elliot and Mick shared a vision at the beginning. Elliot was this creative, passionate and protective guy who, if he is on your side, then the other side is in trouble," recounts Levine, whose view is quite simply that there would never have been a Simply Red if it had not been for Elliot Rashman. Having said that, the producer did have a sense that things were set to change.

"I wasn't surprised when Elliot left. Mick had changed and become abusive during the making of *Life*. He was edgy, confrontational and disrespectful to me but much worse to Elliot, who found his hands tied creatively. He had just had enough."

According to Grenfell, the problems went back as far as the *Life* tour and Japanese dates in 1996 when he saw things begin to crumble. "None of the problems that had built up over the years had been addressed and while everyone thought it was still working, it was in fact getting worse until, finally, it blew up."

The blow-up is confirmed by Dodd who says that he and Rashman had "a bit of a Liam and Noel moment but people move on and that was the end of it." After working together for 13 years – "twelve of them were brilliant; a very intense roller coaster in which we did 25 years worth of work" – the pair who started So What to look after Simply Red went their separate ways.

"Elliot was frustrated with the business and maybe thought things should be going in a different direction," explains Dodd, who describes Rashman as "passionate and protective about Mick and the music" and is full of praise for his ex-partner. "He is a one-off and the world would be a much duller place without people like him. He is a brilliant pop historian, steeped in American contemporary literature and a child of the 60s counter-culture. I always had him down for a North Manchester mix of Alan Ginsberg meets Lenny Bruce – very dry, very funny and people either loved or loathed him."

"There's not a lot to hide about Elliot leaving. I just think he didn't want to do it any more. We were very much in sync, we talked two or three times every day about virtually everything and were very close and I still feel close to Elliot. It was 100% perfect and I never ever fell out with him, he just moved on because he'd had enough.

He had lots of other things to deal with in his own life and he went off and did them. The whole thing between us was thoroughly decent but his main fall-out was with Andy who I had a very tight working relationship with, which I think surprised Elliot.

Andy was doing most of the business while Elliot was more involved in the creative areas, and Elliot jumping ship was one of the things that made me blue and made me reassess my career."

Love And The Russian Winter, again produced by the team of AGM, arrived in the shops a month before the new millennium. Even as it peaked at number six – and the two single releases both failed to break into the top ten – Mick was planning a new career which crucially would leave him in charge of his own destiny.

After this, however, in November 2000, East West released an album which appeared with Mick's knowledge but significantly without his blessing and served only to confirm Mick's worst fears about continuing his career with this major record company. The album *It's Only Love* was a record company compilation which, even with the much discussed 'Ev'ry Time We Say Goodbye', sank almost without trace.

Within a month Mick and Simply Red had said their final, highly publicised and somewhat acrimonious goodbyes to East West Records and Warner Music, and embraced two years with no tours and no records but an awful lot of planning.

While things also came to an end officially with East West in America at the same time, Lisa Barbaris reflects that Simply Red had been on a downward curve in the US for some time. "Neither *Blue* nor *Love And The Russian Winter* did well here. They were really rejected in America and by then the label had sort of lost interest in Mick and Simply Red."

With Rashman gone and the record deal coming to an end, Andy Dodd took the decision to appoint a new partner to help manage Simply Red and the person he chose was a man who had travelled the world with Mick during seven eventful years.

Ian Grenfell had become general manager of East West Records and received *Love And The Russian Winter* as Simply Red's contract was nearing its end. "I listened to the album and knew it wasn't up there – it didn't have any singles on it – and it was clear that Mick had ceded more control to Gota and Andy. But I was still panicking because we might be losing Simply Red, and I seemed to be the only person in the company who was bothered about it."

In the end, instead of just losing Simply Red, East West also lost Grenfell when he agreed to join Dodd in a new company called Silentway which would replace the previous So What Arts operation as the management of Simply Red.

But the fact that he didn't invite Grenfell into the fold sooner still amazes Dodd. "I've always thought that two heads are better than one in this business and I can't believe it took me twelve months to ask Ian into the company after Elliot's departure." He also knew he was getting a new kind of partner after the "roller-coaster years" with Rashman.

"Ian was a perfect choice and very different to Elliot. He is considered, analytical and leads a great team He also has a great dialogue with Mick and commands his respect. He is a gamekeeper turned poacher – both a great record company exec and a great manager."

Sharing a love for Manchester United – and having the foresight to arrange for overseas satellite links so they could all watch their beloved Reds matches wherever they were around the world – made Grenfell's arrival reasonably smooth, but he still knew he was following a tough act.

"I was never going to be another Elliot, although it took more than a year for me to realise that that was what the role was. He was a great manager and a great orator but both Mick and Andy are warm, caring and inspiring people who I trusted implicitly, so it was made easy for me."

The idea the new trio were working on was the formation of a new independent company and label which would be a joint venture between Mick Hucknall, as Simply Red, and Silentway Management.

Long-time manager Dodd first revealed details at the music industry's In The City forum in 2002 when he described the plan as a "fundamental wind-change in the industry." Alongside the central issue of ownership of master recordings, Dodd went on record to explain that the royalty paid to the artists is likely to be anywhere between 200% and 400% higher than under a standard record company contract.

Confirming that the marketing campaign for *Home* and all future Simply Red releases would be in line with any major release, Dodd explained that flexibility would be an extra bonus. "We can pick and choose how we address the world market in a modular fashion and concentrate things in any one territory and then revisit other markets later."

In September 2002 simplyred.com was formed, and Grenfell looks back on two releases by the band's former record label as the driving force behind the new business.

"*It's Only Love* made it clear to us that Warner didn't want a relationship with us, it felt like it was put out to spite us for leaving. And I'm delighted that *Love And The Russian Winter* exists because we wouldn't be here now unless we'd been there. If that album had sold a couple of million, maybe we would have re-signed with East West."

Established to oversee recording, touring, websites and sponsorship activity, simplyred.com was also launched as a possible template for other artists to follow,

as co-manager Andy Dodd told music industry magazine *Music Week* at the time: "This business model offers an alternative way forward for established artists."

"I hope the idea of simplyred.com does shake up the industry. You should get what you pay for. I've got nothing against a record company owning a master recording by an artist who has not paid for the recording. If the company puts up the money and pays for the entire creative process then it's all well and good that they own it. My argument was that we would pay for it, and that they'd own it and that's the bit I can't get my head round.

I said to Andy and Ian that I liked the idea, when we got through the contract, of setting up a little cottage industry. It doesn't matter if we don't sell as many records but I would like to be happy with the records I make and for them to feel natural. I would rather do that, own my work and just sell maybe a million than go through the whole routine with the record company, them owning my master recordings. It was a big risk to the extent that I put my house on the line as security."

Over at EMI Music Publishing, Peter Reichardt watched as Mick's fifteen-year relationship with the Warner Music Group came to a sad end. "At the end I think he got stuffed by Warners, and I didn't like to see it. It all ended acrimoniously and I made my thoughts known. Then he started simplyred.com and everyone said, 'You're mad' but the boy put his hand in his own pocket to do it."

Even if no other artists were to follow suit, Mick stuck to his guns and chased his dream and Reichardt for one is full of admiration. "I take my hat off to him because he then delivered one of the best records he's ever made. He was also on a crusade about owning his own recordings and controlling his catalogue and I'm proud of the fact that EMI were able to hang on to someone like Mick in these circumstances. He might have wanted to start not just his own record company but also his own publishing company."

The idea of this cottage industry had been talked over between the three leading players ever since the band came off the road in May 2000 and following frustrating discussions with some of the world's leading record companies.

"I really loved the idea of the cottage industry but didn't think the industry was quite ready for it," says Grenfell. "If we had the right offer from a major at that time I think Andy and I would have been trying to convince Mick to sign it, but we were trying to sign for a short term basis for a lot of money and the offers on the table were just not right."

Looking with great pride on the decision to create simplyred.com, Dodd describes it as "a milestone for how bands can do business in the 21st century" and confirms that the model for the new business was worked out in partnership with Grenfell once Simply Red were out of their East West contract.

Mick has also shared his views on the ownership of his recordings with many of his friends and colleagues in the music business, among them rock writer

Ian Grenfell and Andy Dodd

Adrian Thrills. "He feels very strongly about the whole copyright issue and the fact that he has a body of work and doesn't own it, and what he did with simpyred.com was a brave move" says Thrills.

"I started to toy with the idea of owning what I had made around the time of making the Blue album. I'd asked Warners for my masters because I'd paid for them and they were basically offering to sell them to me. I said I don't really want to buy them because I already own them, and I still maintain that argument.

I went into the studio and paid for all the costs of making the record, the record company advance is in fact a loan that you have to pay back plus interest and then, when you pay it back, they own it. I believe that I paid for my earlier recordings and that I own them – and one day I will get them back."

"It was also partially a sign of the times, reflecting how the business evolves, and he was pretty much at the forefront of it. In fact he has pushed it further than most and, what is more important to him than the money and profit, is the issue of ownership," add Thrills. "Whether an album sells two million or ten million, in the long term he now owns those records."

So the seeds were sown for Simply Red to pursue independence, and in September 2000 Dodd and Grenfell met Mick in London to give their artist a major PowerPoint presentation that showed all the advantages of going along the do-it-yourself route. "At the end of it Mick just said, 'All those in favour say aye'," recalls Grenfell, "and that was the start of the journey."

With simplyred.com on the launch pad, Grenfell, Dodd and the businessmen set about creating a company that would work while Mick did what he did best. "We had to cost every single thing we wanted to do with every record, plus any other projects, and we created a business model which is still our bible today," explains Grenfell. "While we did this, Mick was off working on the music and around the end of 2001 he announced he'd got the new album."

However, when the new management team heard the new album there was a problem. "When Andy and I heard it we knew it wasn't there, but wondered how we could tell Mick without destroying his creativity," explains Grenfell who, along with Dodd, went to Mick's house for a lunchtime meeting.

"We talked about what needed to happen with the record and in the middle of it, Mick resigned. He said, 'I can't do any better so that's it, sorry'. Because we didn't think the record was good enough, he resigned as Mick Hucknall and announced that he wasn't going to sing any more. We skulked out of his house without even getting lunch."

Recalling the visit to Mick's house for what was meant to be a celebratory meal, Dodd understands the singer's reaction to the comments made by his managers. "He expected a celebration lunch and he was confronted by us going 'sorry, there's just one mile to go'. He had put a lot into it as the first self-owned

release but we wouldn't have been doing our job as managers if we hadn't expressed our view."

"Those conversations are difficult but essentially healthy," says Dodd, who recalls that everybody had recovered their senses within a few hours when Mick called Grenfell on his mobile to explain, "You've got to allow me to be petulant; what do you want me to do?"

Immediately Grenfell and Dodd began talking with Mick about new ideas and working with new people. "Nobody had ever fully A&R'd Mick up until this point. Nobody told him that things were not right or should not be released, which on occasions is what he should have been told over the years, and that became my role," explains Grenfell.

"Releasing the first record was pretty scary," says Grenfell. "The day we released *Home* in April 2003, we were £4 million in the hole and if it didn't work we would have had a problem."

In fact, the crucial factor was the first single 'Sunrise' which proved to be a radio-friendly track and became Simply Red's first top ten hit for nearly five years. The album, which featured Mick, Levine, Gota, Andy Wright and the band's Lewinson brothers as producers, peaked at number two in the UK and produced three more hits including a new successful version of the Stylistics' 1974 hit 'You Make Me Feel Brand New'.

"Once Andy, Ian and I grasped the implications of having our own record company, we suddenly realised that we can actually afford to be more generous in how we deal with our musicians. There is now a broader umbrella and my principles are being served, and I've been empowered to provide a royalty cheque to musicians in perpetuity on one of our records and I'm very proud of that."

Home also represented a significant change in attitude by Mick towards co-writing. While all seven of the new songs on the album featured the name Hucknall in the composer credits, three of them were co-compositions with members of the band, and the last time that had happened was with Fritz McIntyre on *Stars*.

"I've only ever approached Joe Sample and Lamont Dozier to write with me but now we have our own label and company I feel much more relaxed about sharing with the guys I'm working with, and co-writing is one of the things that brings the whole operation together as one."

Having watched anxiously to see how the new album was received, Grenfell was happy with the result. "It did more then we expected. We worked on the principle that if we could do it ourselves and do what Warners did with their last album then that was a result. So when we did twice the previous album we all felt we'd done a very good job."

In this week's issue: BMG and Sony announce merger; MTV Awards wow Edinburgh; Plus: the charts in full

15.11.03/£4.00

MUSICWEEK

CMP
United Business Media

SIMPLY RED
HOME
LIMITED EDITION

LIMITED EDITION ALBUM
FEATURES BONUS DVD
WITH LIVE PERFORMANCES,
DOCUMENTARY FOOTAGE
& 2 EXTRA AUDIO TRACKS
5055131700157

GET HOME FOR CHRISTMAS

The release and success of *Home* is described as a "re-awakening for Mick and Simply Red" by Barbara Charone, a partner with Moira Bellas in MBC PR. "The album and concerts were well-received and what Mick did in moving his career out of a record company and taking control of it brought him a lot of respect and good will."

The story was the same down in Italy, where former Warner man Senardi was now busy running his own NuN Entertainment company, which became home to the new Simply Red album. "The beauty of Mick's voice and his original and unique way of writing are melded with classic soul and R&B," explains Senardi, who was rewarded for his loyalty and commitment with the best-selling international album in Italy in 2003.

Mick's total commitment to his new label and his new album was further confirmed to Grenfell by the singer's new-found enthusiasm for promotion. "In the East West days, anything before midday was early and even midday was often too early for Mick. But when we were in Los Angeles promoting *Home* there was a live radio interview at 7.30am with a wake up call at 6am, and all Mick said was, 'Of course I'm going to do this stuff, it's my label.'"

"There's not a chance I'd go back to a major. I'll do distribution deals but nothing beyond that. I don't see why I should. This is how I will make records for the rest of my career. And most of the people we have working with us are in a similar position of being self-employed so there is a great sense of creativity, freedom and teamwork. I'm not part of the established industry anymore and this allows me to do what I love most, which is communicating with people through music."

The new combination of Mick, Dodd and Grenfell also recruited a team of tried and tested creative people to work on the *Home* project, and most of them were former Warner Music employees, which Dodd views as a major factor in the release of the new album.

"For the release of *Home* we managed to attract a remarkably experienced team of people who had left Warners – Tony McGuinness, Moira Bellas, Barbara Charone and Rainer Focke – and the collective experience was electric as everyone was getting their own back on Warners. It was like signing Manchester United's European Cup winning team on a free transfer!"

Together the team encouraged Mick to such an extent that Dodd, after nearly 20 years of working with Mick, was moved to comment: "I noticed a renewed energy in Mick and all the people around him which I have not seen since the start of Simply Red."

To those who had followed and been linked closely to Mick's career over 20 years, the decision to start his own business still took some getting used to. Publisher Reichardt immediately sensed a new freedom about the singer coupled with a certain apprehension about the level of financial investment, but nothing stood in the way of the creative process.

"He had real belief that *Home* was a great album and he rose to the occasion artistically, creatively and in every way. He knew a lot was hanging on it and because he went very public, a lot of record companies were willing him to fail," explains Reichardt.

Thrills too noticed Mick's commitment to the new company and the new album. "It never felt – in terms of production, promotion or marketing – that *Home* was done on the cheap. They still competed with the big boys and even though it is a cottage industry, it's a cottage industry with a fair amount of muscle."

As one of the architects of the new simplyred.com operation, Dodd sets out the essentials needed to make the cottage industry work efficiently. "It's all about managing risk and being able to gauge efficiently what your minimum potential market will be. Get that right and you know the extent of your marketing budget."

This simple maxim meant that everybody at simplyred.com could react to the demands of the international markets as they responded to the music, but it still required the total support of the artist and according to Dodd, "Mick was entirely supportive and did a massive amount of promotion work around *Home*."

After nearly two years off the road, Simply Red also went back to touring in support of the new album, starting with a week-long residency at Ronnie Scott's club in London. While he was pleased to see Simply Red back on the road, the band's long-time promoter Stuart Galbraith also acknowledged and welcomed the change in the business structure. "The project was quite phenomenal because what Andy, Ian and Mick did was create not only their own recording set-up, but also their own label."

This resulted in what the Live Nation executive describes as "the most productive meetings I've ever had on the set-up of a project in all the years I've been working with the band." All of a sudden there was no agenda other than Simply Red, and there were no concerns about fitting into a record company's release schedule or with other marketing campaigns.

Being able to move singles and albums to fit in with tour dates and having a schedule that doesn't feature any other releases or artist activities made Galbraith's job a lot easier. "In 2005, we were able to do things like moving the tour back a bit and moving the album forward a bit to get that window that ensured that the tour supporting the album sold much better."

All this advance planning came to fruition in October 2005 when Simply Red launched their ninth original studio album entitled *Simplified*.

The essentially unplugged album featured vintage tracks such as 'Holding Back The Years', 'Fairground' and 'Something Got Me Started' with new arrangements alongside three new songs. The idea came, as Grenfell confirms, from the *Classic Album* television programme about *Stars*. "Mick was asked to

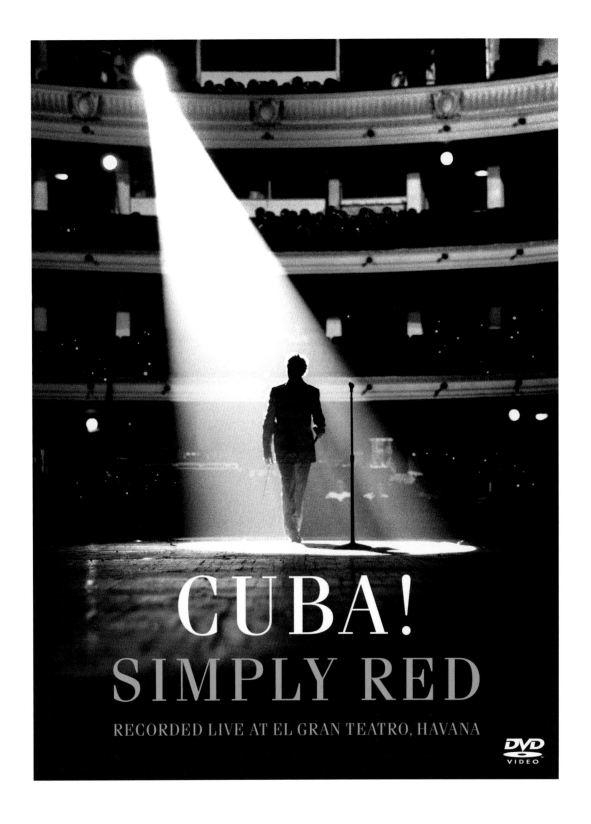

sing three songs acoustically for the programme and everybody was in tears when he did 'For Your Babies'."

The album, supported by a series of UK and European dates, took Mick and the band back into the UK charts at number three, became a top five European best-seller and also heralded an in-concert DVD shot in Cuba which, as Grenfell recounts, was not an easy thing to organise.

"You have to be invited to play in Cuba, so we wrote to the Cuban government saying it was our 20th anniversary and we'd love to play a concert and film a DVD in Cuba. It was all very formal, saying things like, 'We know you've probably never heard of Simply Red but we are a major international act'."

When the reply came, it was from a freelance Cuban fixer who had been given the letter by the authorities and Grenfell was completely taken aback. "This guy Ernesto wrote back saying he didn't see how it could be our 20th anniversary as Mick left the Frantic Elevators in1983. He lived in Havana and was a massive Elevators and Simply Red fan and he helped us sort things so that, in the end, we shot three videos plus the DVD in Cuba."

Working as arranger/conductor on the concert in Cuba was Simon Hale and he flew to the Caribbean island unsure if the local Cuban string players would understand pop music or how they'd interact with the group's rhythm section. "But Cuba has an extraordinary musical culture," he was relieved to discover. "They were absolutely stunning players who played with great passion, astounding tuning and phenomenal rhythm."

The band which has become established as Simply Red and that Mick took with him to Cuba also impressed Hale who, although he worked on the *Home* album, was involved in a live situation for the first time. "They are absolutely top class and if Mick says they are the best band he's ever had, then I certainly wouldn't argue with him."

"This band fulfils the dynamic that's necessary to make the kind of music I want to make. It came about during the making of Home *and we came out of the album with this fantastic band that was so together, so in sync and we're still rising and getting better."*

While Mick's promotion of the new album in America consisted of just one day of telephone interviews, his US manager Barbaris remains confident that he still has an audience in the world's largest music market. "America is still interested in Mick and Simply Red and, while there is no guarantee that if he came here and did 90 shows he would get America back, if he doesn't come here you can be sure it won't happen," is her assessment of the situation.

With over a hundred new records being released in America every week, competition is tough and Barbaris accepts that a major Simply Red tour of

Right: Havana, Cuba, 2005

America would probably end up losing money, but she is still optimistic. "I totally believe that if he did six weeks here he could get America back and it disappoints me personally that I can't deliver America for him – and I'm a little mad about not getting the help I need."

Mick's constant quest for quality coupled with adventure is what makes him such an interesting artist for music journalist Thrills who believes that, while the singer has changed and broadened his interests over 20 years – "and I'd be worried if he hadn't" – one thing has remained the same. "There has been no dilution in his love of music and he has still the same hunger, which is perhaps unusual for someone who's been at it for so long."

The passing of time has also had its effect on the thing that many people consider to be Mick's greatest asset – his extraordinary and wide ranging soulful voice. According to Wright, it has been a change for the better. "His voice nowadays has better tonality and is warmer but probably not as passionate as it was. He was a different man 20 years ago, there was a youthful passion back then. Now he is more contented, more settled and that means a different set of emotions coming out of his body."

As a member of Simply Red for over 20 years, Kirkham has seen musicians, producers and record executives come and go, but there was one specific plan which never even got off the drawing board.

"Around the time of *Life* somebody said I should become Simply Red's musical director," he explains. "I told them there was no such animal in this band but I'll be the guy who remembers what the songs are supposed to go like when we're learning them and who remembers what songs we've done on what tour and from one record to another and how they sounded.

"But at the end of the day Mick's the musical director, he's the artist and he decides how the songs and the records should sound."

"The way we are now we've never had before... where I'm fulfilling a role clearly as a band leader but they are also fulfilling their roles not only as musicians but also by being involved in the making of the record and the style in which we play. Right now I cannot see any weak links, and I'm hoping to make at least two or three more albums with this band and then I don't know what I'll do – maybe call it a day and go fishing!"

THANK YOU

THANK YOU

"Of course I'm proud of getting accolades."

Most million-selling rock stars can produce enough platinum and gold records to fill a good-sized room and the really successful can throw in some music awards to complete the décor, but only a select few can also boast of appearing in the hippest comic on the block or the wittiest satirical puppet show.

Mick Hucknall and Simply Red have collected the platinum and gold records; over 130 of them recognising certified sales from around the world and representing the different levels of sales certification in each country – 300,000 in the UK, one million in the US or just 15,000 in Singapore means another platinum album.

Awards, too, have come his way from fans' polls, national and international music events and even universities but it's never been a one-way street for Mick who has used his fame, good fortune and personality to invest time, effort and money in a wide range of interests stretching from property development and writing songs to creating record companies and supporting charities.

The band's first taste of success in a national poll came in 1985 when *Record Mirror* readers placed them sixth in the list of Acts Most Likely To Succeed. The following year Mick topped *Rolling Stone* magazine's critics' poll as Best New Male Singer while the readers named Simply Red as one of the top two new British bands. *Billboard* went even further and listed Simply Red among the nominations in eight different categories.

A couple of years later, Mick got the call from Diana Ross asking him to write a song just for her and he delivered 'Shine' for her *Red Hot Rhythm 'N' Blues* album and in 1988 he wrote 'I'm Gonna Lose You' which Simply Red performed on the soundtrack to Roman Polanski's movie *Frantic*, starring Harrison Ford.

"I love Diana Ross and when I was asked to write her a song I was absolutely thrilled, I do think she's wonderful. It was a one-off and it was a great experience.

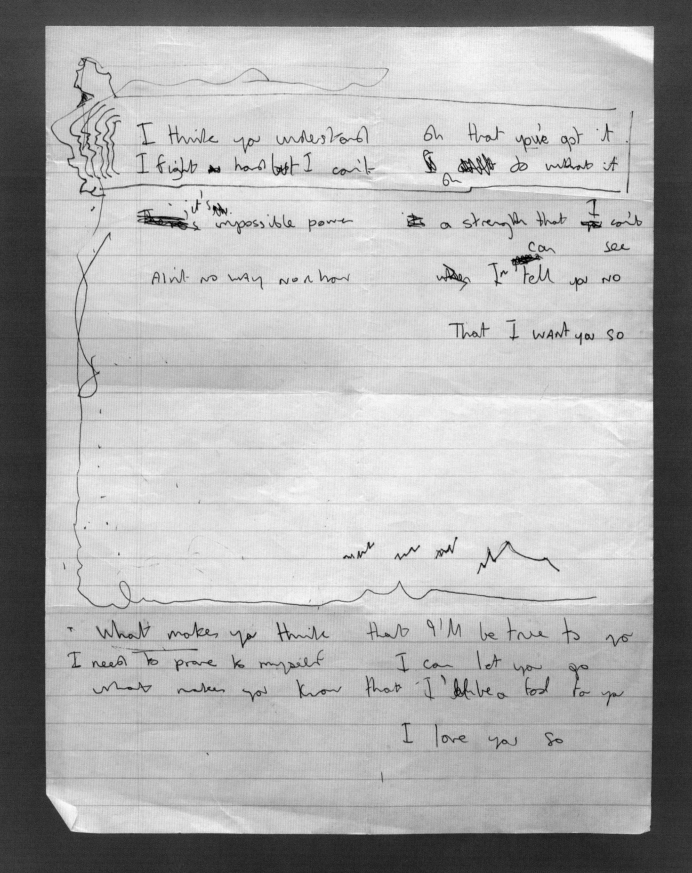

I think you understand   Oh that you've got it

I fight ~~so~~ hard ~~but~~ I can't   ~~It~~ do what it

Oh

~~It's~~ it's ~~an~~ impossible power   ~~It~~ a strength that ~~I~~ can't

can   see

Ain't no way nor how   ~~when~~ I tell you no

That I WANT you so

What makes you think   that I'M be true to you

I need ~~to~~ prove to myself   I can let you go

What makes you know that I'll be a fool to you

I love you so

I was proud to do it for her and she came down to the studio when we were recording to say hello – and she is very beautiful."

The man who looked after Mick's music publishing would have liked this to have been the start of something big, but former EMI Music executive Peter Reichardt remained frustrated by Mick's songwriting habits.

"He's not a prolific songwriter and I don't think there are a lot of unrecorded or unreleased songs lying about. Singing is the easy bit, making a record is slightly harder, songwriting is the really hard part," is Reichardt's theory, but still he would have liked more songs from the Simply Red frontman.

"I would like to see him write songs for other acts because it would be such an easy sell – 'Would you like this great song by Mick Hucknall that no one has heard and he's not recording?' And I'd love him to co-write and get together with people like Guy Chambers or Pharell Williams. They could be really interesting collaborations but Mick is not the sort of writer I could ring up and say, 'Have you got a song for so and so?' He doesn't work like that and I understand that. He writes for himself and his style is unique."

The former keyboard player with Squeeze is a man who appreciates Mick not only as a songwriter but also as a dinner companion. "He's a great writer and has written many great songs," says Holland who, acknowledging that he has been blessed to work with some of the greatest musicians and performers, has noticed that they all have one thing in common. "For the people who have greatness, music is there all the time. Mick is on music all the time. You can go out with him and he's great company because you can talk about all sorts of great music."

"Songwriting doesn't get any easier but I am still absolutely immersed in it. I do tons of lyrics and it's getting peculiarly more like how I imagine maths would be, like creative maths. You've only got a certain amount of bars so how do you make those bars go by without sounding like the previous ones that might have been more interesting?

As I get older this whole scenario goes more into that kind of imaginative maths where you break the random and yet you are still fixed by this metronomic thing. I am fascinated by it and it really is a joy.

Writing for other people is not something I've really pursued aggressively and I don't get that many requests to write for other people. I'm very ambitious regarding my own music and in the last few years I've got very specific, and I try to put all my energies into stuff that I'm going to record."

Despite Reichardt's view, Mick did take up the challenge of co-writing back in 1986 when he worked with Lamont Dozier. As a tribute to the legendary Motown partnership with Brian and Eddie Holland – and their famous songwriting credit of Holland Dozier Holland (on hits for The Supremes, Smokey Robinson, Martha Reeves, Jr Walker, The Four Tops, The Isley Brothers

Left: Mick's handwitten lyrics for 'You've Got It'

Top: With Diana Ross

Bottom: Mick and Jools Holland at *Jools Holland's Annual Hootenanny*, December 2000

and Marvin Gaye) – they created the Hucknall Dozier Hucknall credit for the songs 'Infidelity' and 'Suffer'. He followed-up with two more Hucknall/Dozier compostions – 'You've Got It' and 'Turn It Up' – and then wrote 'Enough' with Crusaders leader Joe Sample.

Dozier has his own recollection of working with Mick. "On the songs we wrote together it was different because we just sort of walked away from it, put it down and talked about the business and went back to it. You can crowd your senses when you try too hard and when nothing came, we got up and walked around and talked about other things."

The exercise seemed to help. "We got some daylight in there and then went back to it." says Dozier.

"Lamont might not look like a greyhound but he writes like one, he's amazing. He just comes up with so many ideas in such a short period of time. You've almost got to act like kind of an editor and say, 'Wait, hold it.' It's amazing and I can see that with Holland and Holland and him it would have been good because it would have been kind of an edit for him – he is just a melodic machine.

When we did 'Infidelity' and 'Suffer' it worked out that when I left Lamont's house there were virtually no lyrics – maybe just two or three lines – and all the melodies were complete. So I went away and formulated more of the melody with the band and got all the lyrics together and sent Lamont our version. We were touring so we couldn't sit down and do it in one place... it was sort of made on the hoof.

Writing with Joe Sample was another fantastic experience but on a completely different level. There's much more of a cerebral, intense expression inside his music and I tried very much to encapsulate the mood that he was in that night while we worked on the song and he was describing the breakdown of his marriage. This riff kept going through him and I started work on that. It was one of those thunder and lightning moments, and I love that song."

The lack of cover versions of Mick's songs is another source of disappointment to Reichardt, who firmly believes that more artists could and should perform his songs. "We have tried over the years with various artists but sometimes songs are unique to an artist and don't really lend themselves to another artist's style.

"For whatever reasons, people do not want to experiment with Mick's songs in the same way that he will with other people's songs. I think that has led to him being grossly underrated as a song-writer."

Another person who thinks Mick's skill as a writer has been overlooked is Adrian Thrills. "People look at him, see the performer, hear the voice and the grooves, see Simply Red the band and sometimes ignore this guy as a writer. But this guy loves The Beatles and has a really good grasp of what it takes to make a really good pop song and that's something that has gone on right through the years."

Top: World Music Award, 1992   Bottom: With Lamont Dozier

116

Receiving multi-platinum sales award from
Max Hole and the Warner Music UK sales team

Be it known that the

National Academy of Recording Arts & Sciences®

has nominated

Simply Red

for outstanding achievement in the category of:

Best New Artist

"Picture Book"

In the 29th Annual Grammy Awards®
and that

So What Arts Limited

has participated

1986

Mick with BRIT Award

"I'm fine with other people covering my songs but I think one of the reasons it tends not to happen is because I am still a contemporary artist. Actually, covers are not much of an issue because we are in the top ten most-played artists in radio history which must mean that people like the versions we've done. There are plenty of artists in America who have done 'Holding Back The Years'. I think it is very much a standard over there and I've even had seven or eight requests from rap acts to do it."

In 1987, Simply Red made their debut appearance on the UK's BRIT Awards show although in those days they were called the British Phonographic Industry Awards, but – despite nominations as Best Group, for *Picture Book* as Best Album and 'Holding Back The Years' as Best Single – they came away empty-handed.

They were similarly rewarded at the 1987 Grammy Awards in America where they were unsuccessfully nominated twice, but still managed to create a stir by appearing without the traditional tuxedo and black tie. Mick's appearance without a tie and reportedly resembling a "crumpled bed" was all part of his stand against the glamour and stardom of the music business.

"We weren't very fashionable or glamorous. The Grammys were more for our aunts than for us. We went loaded with pens and pads to get as many autographs as we could for Aunt Nellie and cousin David back in England."

Three years on and Simply Red were among the nominations for the BRITs with nominations as Best Group, for Best Album with *A New Flame* and 'If You Don't Know Me By Know' as Best Music Video, but again they lost out.

Again, in 1992, they were three-time nominees for Best Group and for Best Album and Best Music Video with *Stars*, but even though they finally made it on to the winner's podium, it was an unsatisfactory night all round.

They were forced to share the Best Group award with KLF in circumstances that certainly outraged their record company boss Max Hole. "I think we said that Simply Red wouldn't be there unless they had actually won something. Then we were tipped off that they had won Best Group but we only found out a few hours before the show that they were sharing it with KLF." While Hole knew that nobody had told him or Simply Red about sharing the prize, he suspected that no one had told KLF about the arrangement either.

"I was furious and both Elliot and Mick were just as angry as me. I gave the BRITs chairman a serious ear-bashing but I don't think anyone ever got an apology or an explanation."

While Mick gave the professional performance expected of him, KLF took the opportunity to fire a dummy machine-gun into the audience during their set and announce their retirement from the music business before dumping a dead sheep at the after-dinner party with the message 'Bon Appetit' pinned to its fleece.

Top: Receiving honorary degree from UMIST   Bottom: Ivor Novello Awards, London, 2002

The upshot was that Mick made it two shows in a row when he appeared at the 1993 BRITs and walked off with awards for Best Male Artist and Best Group alongside a nomination for 'For Your Babies' as Best Music Video.

Simply Red's quick return to the show was not lost on Hole. "He won two awards but being invited on the show again the next year was unusual. It may well have had something to do with people trying to make up for the previous year."

Mick made his fourth BRITs appearance in 1996, putting him behind only Robbie Williams (including his Take That years) in the list of most live performances on the UK music industry's premier awards shows. He sang 'Fairground' which was among the nominations for Best Single and Best Music Video.

Even before the BRITs came on to the scene, Simply Red contributed to a significant Grammy victory in America when the band's 1989 hit version of 'If You Don't Know Me By Now' earned writers Kenny Gamble and Leon Huff the 1990 prize for Best Rhythm & Blues Song.

A year on and Mick and Moss were honoured as composers of 'Holding Back The Years' and collected an ASCAP (American Society of Composers Authors & Publishers) award for the song's broadcast success in America.

In 1992, after collecting a World Music Award in Monte Carlo, Mick was honoured for his songwriting when he was awarded the prestigious Ivor Novello Award as Songwriter of the Year and the following year a combination of *Daily Mail* readers and Radio 1 listeners voted *Stars* number 1 in a poll of the 100 Best Albums.

The MOBOs (Music of Black Origin) honoured Mick in 1997 for making an Outstanding Achievement to Music and this was followed by an honorary Masters degree, awarded by UMIST in recognition of Mick's "contribution to life in Manchester, fund-raising in the wake of the bomb (the IRA bombed Manchester city centre in1996) as well as his outstanding contribution to British and Manchester's music success worldwide."

In 2002 and 2003 Mick added to his trophy cabinet with two awards which recognised his extraordinary musical talent. The Capital Radio Award was for his Outstanding Contribution to Music, while his skill as a songwriter was at the heart of his prestigious Ivor Novello Award for an Outstanding Song Collection.

The "Ivors" – as they are affectionately known – recognise the art and skill of composers alongside the success of songs and are voted for by fellow composers and music industry experts. They hold a unique position within the British music industry which *Music Week* editor-in-chief Martin Talbot touched on in a 2002 comment column. "It is an award show which refuses to be led by fashion, to the extent that it is almost anti-fashion, as shown by the awards for EMI's much missed Kate Bush and the label-less Mick Hucknall."

As a publisher, Reichardt knows full well what an 'Ivor' means to a songwriter. "The Ivor Novello awards seem to have a weight that the BRITs do not. I think Mick's award was better late than never because he is very underrated as a vocalist, for his musical output, and most importantly, for his songwriting."

"The awards that give me greatest pleasure are the Ivor Novellos. Songwriting awards get to me personally and are the ones that really count, they are very special.

I don't give a toss about the BRITs. There have been times when I've known full well what the politics are within the record companies and I've just stood there feeling frustrated. I don't have respect for them, they've not earned my respect and they shouldn't get the respect of most musicians because they just capitalise on the back of us.

When Simply Red and KLF shared the BRIT Award I said to KLF that I'd rather they had it, I didn't want to share it with them. I wanted to give it to them and they wanted to give it to me but we both just hated the organisers for doing it to us.

Neither of us was told we were sharing it and both of us were just pissed off about it. Bill Drummond wanted to do something mad on stage and what he did was genius – I love Bill.

At the end of the day, awards mean you smile, thank somebody and walk off."

In 2004 the efforts of the newly launched simplyred.com organisation were also recognised and rewarded by the British music industry when, for their "ground-breaking structure", the company was awarded the UK Achievement Award by industry magazine *Music Week*.

Ever willing to lend a helping hand, Mick gave his support to Princess Diana's Aids charity when he appeared at the Concert of Hope at Wembley in 1993 alongside George Michael and k.d. lang, and a decade later he was helping actor/producer and patron Kevin Spacey at the Unite For The Future event at London's Old Vic theatre.

On a more personal level, he was involved in Eric Cantona's farewell game for Manchester United in 1998, and a year later found himself singing at United manager Alex Ferguson's testimonial event.

However, Mick's love and association with Manchester stretches further than Old Trafford and the red shirts of United. He has never forgotten his roots and when success provided him with the opportunity to do something positive he grabbed it with both hands and, according to Andy Spinoza, he put some other famous Mancunians to shame.

"Oasis are supposedly the hip and popular sons of Manchester but they took all their money, left Manchester and never put a penny back into it. Mick, on the other hand, helped regenerate the city centre and played an

HER ROYAL HIGHNESS
THE PRINCESS OF WALES

concert of

Hope

A unique concert for:
World AIDS Day

In the presence of **HER ROYAL HIGHNESS
THE PRINCESS OF WALES**

at **WEMBLEY ARENA
WEDNESDAY
1st DECEMBER 1993**

All proceeds from this
concert will be donated to:

national aids trust

CRUSAID
The National Fundraiser for Aids

Featuring **GEORGE MICHAEL**

With Special Guests **MICK HUCKNALL**

k.d. lang

PRODUCED BY
THE ROD GUNNER ORGANISATION
FOR GREENHURST PRODUCTIONS LTD

Princess Diana, Mick and George Michael,
Concert of Hope, Wembley, 1993

important part in this development and hasn't got the credit he deserves for what he's done."

"I wanted to be an active part of the revitalisation of Manchester and wanted to give something back to the city. Apart from my music I'm probably more proud of that than anything else. It has been wonderful but the people around me are not big on self-promotion, that's not what we did it for. Ultimately it speaks for itself, it will be there as an entity and show what we did – I don't need to tell people about it."

"This is a guy who was born on Deansgate – the main street in Manchester," says Dodd, who has been associated with Mick for over two decades, "and he's not lost that. Manchester is his spiritual home."

Another investment is one which, while it might not be the most profitable item in Mick's portfolio, does have a place close to his heart. Blood And Fire is a record label which specialises in his beloved reggae music.

Started in 1993, it's based in Manchester and run by Bob Harding, who shares Mick's love of reggae which for so long dominated journeys on the Simply Red tour bus. With Rashman's and Dodd's support for both the music and the business plan, Blood And Fire emerged ten years after the birth of the compact disc.

"There wasn't very much good, well-presented reggae out on CD," explains Harding, "so the original idea was get the rights to a couple of classic reggae albums, clean up the sound, present it really well and put them out so they were on a par with the best jazz, soul and R&B re-issues."

Those first two albums were *Heart of the Congos* by the Congos and Burning Spear's *Social Living,* and from there things grew with the help of reggae historian and compiler Steve Barrow, who travelled to Manchester for a meeting with Mick and Harding. "At the end of that meeting we decided we would actually start a label, make it an ongoing thing and licence all the classic Jamaican reggae that wasn't already available on CD."

After ten years of financial and moral support, Mick put together a celebration Blood And Fire compilation album and he threw himself into the task. "It was entirely his choice of tracks," says Harding. "It was a collection of his favourites, assembled in the order he wanted and, having been a DJ, he knows how to do a running order."

In 2004 the label released its first new recordings but as yet Mick has not appeared on a Blood And Fire release, preferring to keep his playing to a guest spot as bassist on a solo dub album by fellow dub reggae fan and former Simply Red drummer Gota. "Having Mick play bass was great. We always shared this love of dub, talked about it all the time on tour and even used to go shopping for records in the afternoons before a show."

"The inspiration for Blood And Fire was wanting to fly the flag for dub art – that's the bottom line really. I just wanted to spread the message. It's something that has been a huge influence on musicians and a lot of artists, but it's somehow not really been brought into the public domain in a big way.

I think we've done that very well and we now have a superb catalogue. I'm very proud of Blood And Fire which really has been a labour of love because I've certainly not made any money out of it. I've been financing it for over ten years at a loss but I just wanted to show the world that genre of music and all that goes with it."

Together with his Japanese percussionist, Mick also added another string to his bow when the pair re-mixed Björk's 1993 top 30 hit 'Venus As A Boy'.

Alongside Mick's love of music comes a love of food and as a chef of some skill he jumped at the chance in 1996 to be a judge on television's *Masterchef* programme. His appreciation of food sits alongside an investment in wine and a devotion to most things Italian which has developed and been refined over the years, and Stefano Senardi has been a close observer of Mick's life in Italy.

"In a way his international career started in Italy and he has spent so much time in the country over the past 20 years that he is loved by three generations of fans – both men and women."

His friends at the Italian record company spotted Mick's well known affection for members of the opposite sex and at a party in Italy to celebrate his birthday they gave the singer an unusual but – they thought – appropriate present.

"We gave him a big box with a live turkey inside. When he opened it he was very scared. We always called him 'tacchino' which is Italian for turkey, but is also a word we use for somebody who likes girls very much."

Extending his connection with Italy, Mick developed the vineyard in Sicily that he mentions below and nursed his grapes to fruition on the volcanic soil of Mount Etna. After a successful harvest in 2001, he presented the first vintage of Il Cantante – "The Singer" – Etna red wine, known locally as Simply Red. It was dubbed as "excellent with a robust structure" by Sicily's agricultural authority.

"Italy is a place I love – it is my second home. The people are very passionate about us and sometimes I think we are more popular there than here in the UK. Now I've got my vineyard up and running and we've made our first wine which is all very exciting. I did think I should have a basic understanding of grapes and vintages but didn't spit out all I tasted. Who would when what's being poured costs over £200 a bottle?"

Since first seeing and interviewing Mick in the 1980s, writer Adrian Thrills has kept a keen eye on proceedings over the past two decades and has noticed a few changes. "He has a love of life, a thirst to absorb things. In the early 1980s

Mick presents Il Cantante to Pope John Paul II
prior to concert at the Vatican, December 2004

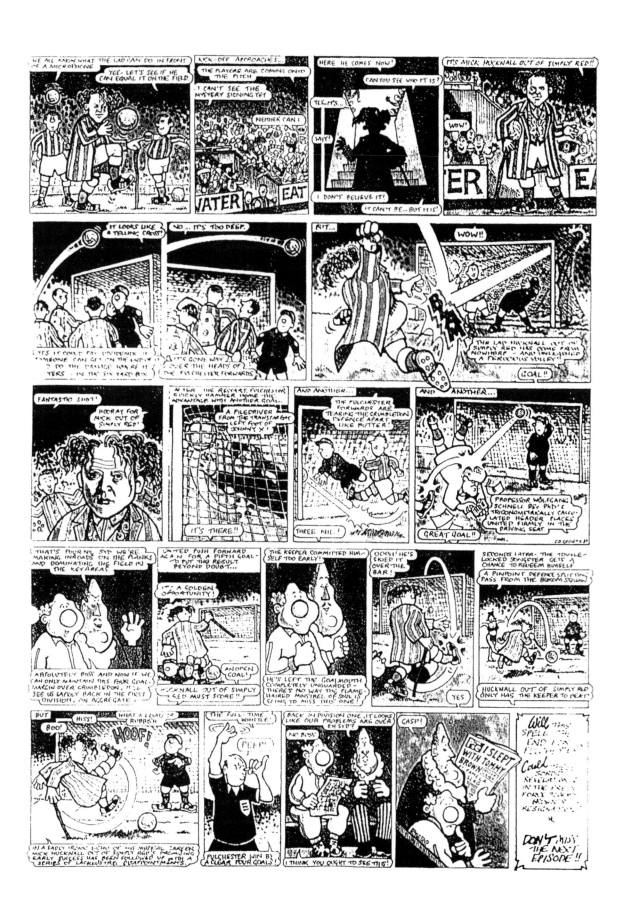

when I first met him it was mainly music obviously, but since then he has moved on and now he loves his wines and he loves cooking."

However, it's not just in Italy that Mick has been recognised and rewarded. For the past decade, the IFPI (International Federation of Phonographic Industries) have handed out platinum awards for albums released from 1996 onwards which have sold a million copies in Europe. So far Simply Red have collected a total of nine – three each for *Life* and *Greatest Hits* and single awards for *Blue*, *Love And The Russian Winter* and *Home*.

But even when you've sold more than ten million records in Europe in the past ten years and a total of over 15 million in the UK – which means you are in the top 30 list of all-time British chart acts – there are still things that cannot be measured in terms of sales figures and chart positions.

And so it is with Mick who, in 1989, was given a special place in history when he featured in a Billy The Fish story in the irreverent and hugely popular comic *Viz*. They took to calling him 'the flame-haired minstrel of soul' and in the famous football comic strip bizarrely teamed him up with Shakin' Stevens as Fulchester United's striking partnership.

And if that wasn't enough, a couple of years later, he "appeared" as a puppet in the groundbreaking television series *Spitting Image* which so memorably satirised Margaret Thatcher and Ronald Reagan.

"I used to buy Viz *so I was a fan and I got a particular thrill because they sent me two annuals with original drawings in them which will be collector's items one day. I just thought it was funny – nice and Northern with good humour. I think of* Spitting Image *as more of a compliment than anything as we'd only just arrived just as* Spitting Image *was tailing off. The fact that they got me in made me a piece of this wonderful satirical history which I just thought was incredible."*

Left: *Viz* comic, 1989

Top: *Spitting Image* puppets of Mick, Lisa Stansfield and Andrew Strong

127

LIFE

LIFE

"Politics and music are a very dangerous mix."

With music firmly embedded in his soul, Mick's thoughts, like those of many a Mancunian before him, turned to football and then, not surprisingly for a working class lad with a bright and inquisitive mind, to politics.

Mick's interest in the political situation in the United Kingdom in the 1970s of Prime Ministers Edward Heath, Harold Wilson and James Callaghan developed, according to his dad Reg, with the arrival of a lodger.

"Bill was a drinking pal whose wife had left him and he wanted a spare room for a couple of weeks. It turned out to be a couple of years but the money was handy and he was quite an academic so he helped Mick with his school stuff."

Mick was in his early teenage years when Bill arrived in the house and, together with Reg, he began to influence the youngest man in the house. "I probably influenced him a bit, I always voted Labour," says Mick's dad, "but he got more about politics off Bill, who was a real leftie and very politically minded."

By the time he was at college Mick was getting pulled in a different direction, and this time it was Alf Spike who was debating politics with the teenager. According to Nellie, her husband was swinging towards the Tory Party and away from the Labour Party he had always supported, but whose new left-wing policies he was firmly against.

"They had long discussions about politics and didn't see eye to eye all the time but it never got aggressive. I think Mick had a lot of respect for Alf and he listened and took it all in before making up his mind about things."

While Alf might have been swinging to the right, Mick was developing his firmly held support for the Labour Party, but Nellie recalls that her husband really didn't want Mick to get involved with politics at all, particularly when singing for a living became an option. "He used to say, 'Stick to what you're doing now, you'll do well with your voice.' He never thought Mick should mix politics with his music."

Right: Johnny Hallyday, Sean Penn, Mick and Bono

Members of Labour Government Councils and Forum.
Clockwise: Mick, Sir Colin Southgate, Chris Smith, Steven Daldry,
Peter Mandelson, Sir Gerry Robinson, Sir Richard Eyre, Stewart Till,
Alan McGee and Sir Terence Conran. *Frank Magazine,* June 1998

"Mixing music and politics has done me a lot of harm within the media but I have to stand up for my principles. I believe in basic Labour principles and as much as people can criticise Tony Blair, they've actually done what it says on the tin. We've got less than a million unemployed, we've got inflation at under 2%, we've never before had this amount of wealth within the working class – so much so that the working classes no longer call themselves working class anymore. "

However, it was at a music event that Mick first met the Prime Minister-in-waiting. At the 1992 BRITs, where he was collecting awards for the *Stars* album, Mick met Tony Blair who was among the new breed of politicians who saw such events as part of their image-building process. On the back of this meeting, Mick was invited to speak at a Labour Party conference and soon put his money where his mouth was by donating a reported £50,000 to the party's coffers.

Blair repaid some of Mick's support and loyalty when he was asked to select his favourite singles of 1996 by rock paper *New Musical Express*. Stressing that the list was not in order of preference, he picked party supporters Oasis alongside Simply Red's 'Angel' and explained. "By coincidence, Mick Hucknall is another strong supporter of the Labour Party... he's had a good year and this is the best of a good bunch."

"Tony Blair and I just started talking and we hit it off well and because of my beliefs I decided to give my support. I was happy to help out during his leadership campaigns and whatever I've done it's been for what I believe is the good of the country. Showing support doesn't just mean a financial gesture. I admit that I have sent notes to Tony Blair from time to time and that he has replied – but it's private correspondence. Some people misinterpret my involvement and think I have political ambitions... but I don't."

While he consistently maintained that a life in politics was not on his "jobs wanted" agenda, Mick continued to tread the dangerously thin line between music and politics with his highly visible and very vocal support for the Labour Party. Appearances on BBC TV's *Question Time* and at an Oxford Union debate were followed by him agreeing to host some of Alastair Campbell's one-man shows when the former Number 10 press secretary went on the road.

In fact, Campbell's view of rock musicians getting involved with politics has been changed by Mick, together with the likes of Bono and Bob Geldof, but for different reasons. "I think it may be a dangerous area to mix the two but it doesn't really matter. When I first met Geldof and Bono there was definitely part of me that had a sort of resistance to these pop stars coming in and telling us what we should do," says the former media adviser to Prime Minister Blair. "But what made it different was that they had a real depth of knowledge and obvious commitment. I now have a lot of time for them and think they've done a good job."

His support for Mick stems from an even deeper sense of commitment on the singer's part. "Mick is an avowed Labour supporter, even when it wasn't very fashionable and I've always had a soft spot for those who were there when it was all crap. I have never doubted that his support was sincere and that he would always be involved as much or as little as he or we thought was appropriate," explains Campbell.

Understanding that Mick's heart lies with Labour and "always will", Campbell also acknowledges Mick's awareness of politics and how it works for a celebrity. "He is genuinely interested in politics and there's never been any danger that he didn't understand there were limits to what he could do and how much he could be involved."

"Mistakes have been made but I'll support them for the rest of my life. I would be amazed if I ever changed my views and I'd be quite happy to see Gordon Brown follow Tony Blair. I think historically Tony Blair will be known some day as somebody who has done a remarkable job for this country. The one thing that neither the media nor anyone else can ever dispute is my consistency.

I went to Labour Party HQ to implore them to reinstate Ken Livingstone and have him under the Labour flag as Mayor of London. Taking him out of the party was a mistake because Ken is just a Labour man with different views to Tony Blair and we should allow him to have those different views.

I look at politics as being in a party but you don't necessarily have to completely agree."

In 1998, Mick got more involved when then-Culture Minister Chris Smith invited him to be part of a new twelve person advisory committee – the Music Industry Forum – which was charged with advising the government about the music industry. Ironically he sat alongside Dickins – the former head of WEA UK who turned him down and then inherited his contract – who was then head of the British Phonographic Industry.

Debating and deciding what Mick does outside music is a tricky area for co-manager Ian Grenfell but he is well aware of the potential pitfalls. "When we've done research it shows that as many people like his political views as don't like them, but also that even people of the same political persuasion often don't like seeing pop stars talking about politics."

With that warning ringing loud and clear, the final decision is that, while he is promoting a record, Mick usually will steer well clear of the political arena. But, as Grenfell points out, Mick has strong allegiances and there will be times when he breaks the rules.

"Alastair Campbell is a friend of Mick's and when he asked Mick to help with his tour, Mick put friendship over promotion. He's very loyal in that way and it would have been hard for me to say, 'Mick, don't help your friend', and there

will be other times in the future when he wants to do things to help somebody... and he'll do it."

Going out on the road with Campbell during his much-heralded *Audience With...* tour in fact only involved Mick doing two shows – one in his hometown of Manchester and one in Guildford, near his home in Surrey.

"We drove to the show in Manchester and pretty much talked about politics all the way there," recalls Campbell. "He chaired that one and obviously enjoyed it because he agreed to do the one in Guildford, but said he'd only do it if we arrived in his Ferrari because, according to him, 'That would get up people's noses.'"

"I gave Alastair my support because he had a rough time from the media. He did a great job presenting Tony Blair to the media and he's got a great sense of humour. Being in the chair for his shows on tour was fun and I tried to be as neutral as I could and just control proceedings, although I did probe him a couple of times when I didn't think he answered the questions."

Campbell also remembers that in the front row at the show in Guildford was a woman who made it clear that she had turned up just to see Mick. "There was certainly one person there who was a fan of him rather than me... in fact I'm not sure there were any fans of me there at all."

Like many an accomplished and caring songwriter, Mick has been moved to use politics and political situations as a theme for songs even if the right message didn't always get across. His Euro '96 anthem 'We're In This Together,' wasn't written about football or for a football match but had it's origins in South Africa's apartheid history.

"'We're In This Together' is really not about football but about South Africa, and when you listen to it in context it's about understanding that if you don't realise you're in this together then there's going to be a civil war and it's going to be terrible.

The organisers of Euro '96 gave me a brief that when we played in the stadium that day people should become more unified. It was pretty fiery at that time with some elements of hooliganism, and they wanted a solemn, anthemic piece which would calm people down.

I have bittersweet feelings about it being used on that day because when you look at the political situation the song is very poignant. I was saying something about a subject that I feel passionately about and having Hugh Masekela playing and conducting the choir was really a great moment for me, but it got lost, which was sad. We allowed ourselves to get swept up in it all in the cause of promoting a record although Tony Blair remarked that he loved the song – politicians and us are all in this together."

Similarly, Mick's 1991 song 'Wonderland' from the *Stars* album had a point to make about Britain under Margaret Thatcher in the 1980s.

Top: Tony Blair, Mick and Bill Clinton, G8 Summit, May 1998

Bottom: *An Audience With Alistair Campbell,* Yvonne Anaud Theatre, Guildford, 2004

"'Wonderland' is probably the most political song I've written. It was inspired by the lie of getting people to own their own houses when the interest rate was at something like 4% and a year later upping it to 15%. It crippled people, especially small businesses – they were lied to by the Conservative Government. It's a song that makes the point that after twelve years of Thatcher there was only a handful of rich bastards like me who could say they were honestly better off. That did leave me embarrassed."

At the same time, Campbell holds out the opportunity for Mick to compose a political anthem for the Labour Party – but without committing the party to actually adopting it! "In 1997 we had D:Ream and 'Things Can Only Get Better', in 2001 we had 'Lifted' by The Lighthouse Family and last time U2's 'Beautiful Day'," he says, "and if Mick wanted to write one for us, we'd love to hear it.

Football loomed large in Mick's life from an early age and his choice between United or City was made easy early on when George Best, Bobby Charlton and Denis Law wore the red of Manchester United, although after the glory years of the 1960s they suffered a decade of bad results in the 1970s.

"He fell out with United when they got rid of Georgie Best," explains his dad Reg. "Then he took up supporting City for a while but he went back to United. I was more of a racing man than a football fan but Mick had an interest in football like most kids, playing in the street and that, but then he went through a phase when he wasn't interested when he went to Art School."

But there was never any doubt that Mick would return to football and once again place his allegiance firmly with the Red Devils. Mick's association with Old Trafford and Manchester United also includes a close personal friendship with manager Sir Alex Ferguson, which began when they met at Mick's 1992 show at the Old Trafford home of Lancashire Cricket Club.

"Football was always there for me, I'd be playing out in the street all the time. I went to my first Manchester United game when I was eight and I'm still a huge fan and will remain one forever, but I like seeing City win too. I'd love to see Manchester City come second every year – behind United! I am a privileged fan. A club attracts dignitaries and people from the society around them, and my success and investment in Manchester has opened doors that it should quite rightly open.

You got a buzz from being at Old Trafford and seeing Matt Busby around the place. He was a walking piece of history. I was a George Best worshipper – he was the first footballing pop star and I was absolutely gutted when it went pear-shaped for him. He was a hero to us and he had pop star qualities with the hair, the cars and the women.

Later on I used to socialise with Eric Cantona who was a wonderful man with a curious nature. He always asked a lot of questions, and in all honesty I was a little bit in awe of him when I first met him."

Top: Mick and Stanley Matthews at European Football Championships, Wembley Stadium, 1996

Bottom: With George Best

Mick and Sir Alex Ferguson

"Because he is a big Reds fan, he was apparently keen to meet me," recalls Sir Alex Ferguson, "and since then we have become very good friends and I've called him a few times when he's been troubled."

In fact, when Manchester United went through a spell of bad results in late 2005 Mick was busy sending daily messages to Sir Alex. "He sent me a text every day saying, 'We love you, we're behind you and we support what you're doing,' and then when we beat Chelsea his text was about three pages long."

"I think Sir Alex Ferguson sees my achievement and I certainly see what Alex has achieved, and I have a huge admiration for him. I met him when he first joined the club and we've got on ever since. He has become a very dear friend and somebody who has been very supportive of me throughout difficult times privately. He is a great person.

We talk about football, wine and music – and probably in that order. He loves his music, he loves melodic music especially but he likes a bit of rock 'n' roll – Jerry Lee Lewis and all that – but he's got broad tastes and is a very cultured man."

While he is a mutual friend of both Ferguson and Mick, Alastair Campbell can't remember how and when he first met the singer – "It was probably at a Labour party event, it certainly wasn't through music as I'm not a music person" – but he acknowledges that Mick's music did feature in his life before politics, Blair and New Labour.

"When I had a nervous breakdown in1986, one of the things that made my partner Fiona realise it was all going pear-shaped was the fact that I used to come home at night, usually pissed out of my head, and put on 'Money's Too Tight To Mention' by Simply Red and just play it again and again and again."

At the time, Campbell and his partner were living in a ground floor flat in Belsize Park, and not surprisingly his nearest neighbour was less than impressed with what was going on upstairs. "The guy who lived below used to come up and plead with me to stop playing the record," recounts Campbell. "I was on the edge at the time and told him, 'Look you just have to understand I have to do this.' It was interesting therapy."

In addition to football, Mick's friendship with Ferguson is also based on their support for Labour, which Sir Alex describes as "another bond between us which comes from our backgrounds." The long-serving football manager also reckons the fact that father Reg has never changed over the years accounts for son Mick's attitude.

"Despite success and cars and houses, Mick has not really changed. Success can affect you in different ways – the restaurants you use and things like that – and it can put you in an unenviable position with a lot of people, but basically Mick's feet have never left the ground."

With Eric Cantona, 1996

Mick and Jack Nicholson with cast of
Voyeurz musical, London, 1996

*"I don't get hassled in the street and generally speaking people are very nice –
they are my security guards as far as I am concerned. If you make friendly music
you meet pretty friendly people; at the very least making friendly music causes some
people to be indifferent."*

While there is no question that Mick has enjoyed and continues to enjoy the
trappings of fame and fortune, stories of the odd tantrum and a degree of
animosity towards the media have never been far below the surface.

He has never been comfortable with intrusion into his private life and
indeed has continued to be amazed and occasionally angered at people's
fascination with his relationships, politics and opinions. And, as he has often
made his feelings about such things very public, there has been a price to
pay with the media.

Mick understands that being a multi-million-selling international rock star
makes you public property and that is acceptable... but only up to a point.
He knows that being stopped for an autograph or photo goes with the
territory and has never really suffered badly at the hands of the public.

*"I try my best to be part of the celebrity thing but can't feel comfortable with it.
It's all a fake, a façade and I can't be who I'm not. And I accept that the media and
other people will have a pop at me because I won't be part of it. If I had dealt with
the media differently and played a different game I don't think I would have the
integrity I have. There are people out there who have not won anything and yet they
are famous for being a celebrity. I am trying to carve out a niche where I don't have
to play that game, but the media are so powerful they can break me at any time.*

*I prefer to conduct myself in private and I like Mick Jagger for that. For all his
gallivanting in the 1980s, the pictures were all of him arriving at or leaving clubs.
There weren't pictures of him at home with his family or talking about his marriage
break-up and I don't want any of that shit. I have a private life and if I don't have a
private life then I don't have a life. My life has become public but from nothing that
I've said, and that's part of the game. But I'll survive."*

With the unique experience of working with Mick both at his record company
and now as his co-manager Grenfell has seen, both at first hand and around the
world, the whole business of celebrity spotting. "It was all so big back around
Stars that when Mick went through an airport it was a really big deal. But he
always dealt with it pretty well," explains Grenfell.

"There was a shield he put up which didn't really encourage people to come
up and have a chat or try to get involved. He did autographs and photographs
quite happily. Having said that, he takes care of himself and there'll never be a
whole entourage of security men around him. He doesn't need them."

From the time that he first met Mick in the early 1980s, Andy Spinoza has
continued to take an interest in Mick's career, and as a former journalist turned

Top: Prince's Trust Gala Evening, March 2006   Bottom: State Banquet at Buckingham Palace,
March 2005

Top left: Mick with Kate Moss   Bottom left: Stella McCartney   Top right: Spike Lee   Bottom right: Elton John

Mick with the Jagger familiy

public relations man he understands the fine line he treads with the media and those who take issue with his music and his politics.

"Mick has always been himself and never cared about upsetting or offending people," he explains. "He was never keen on playing the game and sometimes that has come out in the media as stories of rudeness or arrogance."

According to Barbara Charone, the person still most closely involved in his PR activities, Mick remains very much his own man. "All things that are annoying about Mick are the things that make him Mick," she declares. "That includes his independent streak. But he's a survivor and people like that about him."

As a journalist who has championed the music of Simply Red, Adrian Thrills also acknowledges that Mick plays the game by his own rules but is driven by a huge desire. "When he made his first album and played those first gigs there was a drive to better himself and to get out of where he was at the time. That drive is still there but now it's about pleasing himself while still producing good music."

"I know he hasn't got any kids but it's like Bono says, 'I couldn't be in a band that my kids thought were crap,' and Mick has this great urge not to become bland."

Spinoza goes further and suggests that Mick has never really been affected by people criticising him or making insulting remarks about his looks or his music. "Those barbs don't actually bother him and really stardom has not changed him in any way. He was just as stroppy and self-assured before he ever became famous. It's still, 'I'm me, take me or leave me'."

Record executive Max Hole takes the view that maybe Mick's attitude and single-mindedness about his music and his career has left him and his band somewhat unappreciated. "Over a ten-year period from the mid-1980s I don't think there was any British act that was as consistently successful as Simply Red. But the interesting thing is that they never really got the critical acclaim for it, the media never really embraced them, they were never really cool. But during that time they were in the list of the top three British acts around the world and people didn't give him the credit he deserved."

Over and above his abiding love of music Mick's wide range of interests – including cooking, wine, films, football, art, motor racing and politics – have also brought him into contact with a wide range of other famous people ranging from childhood heroes to superstar celebrities and, on more than one occasion, royalty.

Mick's support for the Prince's Trust brought him into contact with Prince Charles while his meetings with Queen Elizabeth II were at receptions celebrating the restoration of Windsor Castle and the Queen's Golden Jubilee.

At the first introduction at Windsor in 1998 the conversation reportedly centred around the Queen summing up Mick's career with the words, "So you sing and make wine. How lovely!"

"I think people are living their lives short if you don't have a broad menu in your life, and that includes everything about life."

His affection for the stars of Manchester United is understandable and obvious but throughout the years spent as a global rock star he has also come across a wide range of people who have become buddies and all these influences and relationships are cherished by the young man who grew up in a down-at-heel part of Greater Manchester.

"When I first met Ringo Starr I was awestruck and just thought, 'That's a Beatle, a piece of my life, a piece of my childhood.' And rolling a joint for Keith Richards was one of my great moments. I still idolise people like him for the work they've done and what they represent. He IS rock 'n' roll and Mick Jagger is a musical icon and I look on them as people to look up to and be influenced by."

While Mick knows what it takes to write a song, make a record and to perform in front of thousands of fans, nowadays he also understands what's needed to run his own business interests. But at the end of the day – despite his many other loves and interests – music remains Mick's true passion which, according to his great friend Sir Alex, is just as well.

"He joined us for a training session at Barcelona's ground once and he really does not have the legs to be a footballer," says the legendary football manager, "Let's just say that he chose the right profession with singing!"

"I can't be without music, I need it all the time. Oh, and have you ever heard Sir Alex sing?"

At opening of Bash nightclub. Clockwise:
Dennis Hopper, Thierry Klemeniuk,
Johnny Depp, Mick, Timothy Hutton,
Robin Wright and Sean Penn, Miami 1993

TURN IT UP

TURN IT UP

"I look at it now like making paintings. I look at the mixing desk and just think there are the colours, there's the canvas... now get on with it."

Even though Mick and his band of musicians had all spent time in the studio, getting together in 1985 to make the band's debut album within weeks of signing their first record deal represented a sense of arrival for Simply Red.

Now they were going to be playing with the big boys. Making their records in major studios with a big-time producer who had a serious track record – and who was going to take a percentage of whatever their album made.

"I remember Simon Potts coming forward with the suggestion of Alex Sadkin as producer for the first album but apparently he wasn't available and then Stewart Levine came onto the scene. I knew him from his work with the Crusaders, Womack & Womack and Lamont Dozier. He was a great choice and I don't have any regrets about that at all."

Andy Dodd views the arrival on the Simply Red scene of producer Stewart Levine as one of the most significant events in the band's history. "You cannot underestimate the influence Stewart has had on establishing them as an international act. He is an accomplished old-school producer who knows how to make songs into great records, which is a dying art. He is an R&B player who commands respect among his peers and is also a great human being."

Although Max Hole was at WEA UK, he had little or nothing to do with the first album. "Elektra did the whole thing, they got Levine in and we just put it out and had a hit with 'Money's Too Tight To Mention'. The ball started rolling from there."

Having been chosen as producer after his initial meetings with Potts, producer Levine took the band to Holland to record at the SoundPush Studios in Blaricum and there they worked on the first set of songs for the new album – but not everything was to Levine's liking.

simply red

holding back the years

"The horn section came along and somehow, with overdubs and reverbs, I was able to use them on the album, but it wasn't great." Levine was even less impressed with the band's guitarist. "Dave Fryman was unfortunately way out of his league, he just couldn't cut it. The guitar was crucial to the sound so after a couple of songs I told Elliot that he was a weak link."

Although he was credited for his work on 'Red Box', Fryman was replaced in the group and on the album artwork by a new player who came straight out of Levine's address book. "Sylvan had been in a band called the Untouchables that I had worked with and I had him play on 'Money's Too Tight To Mention'. He was terrific and then Mick recruited him for the band."

"Working with Levine wasn't at all difficult, we all admired and respected him so we listened to his advice. He made some changes to the band and to be completely honest I think it was a case of him thinking people weren't up to it and me basically agreeing with him.

He also opened up the keyboard and brought in Sylvan on guitar halfway through. He could see that Fritz was a very important musician in the band so the emphasis went on his keyboard more than any other instrument."

Recording moved from Holland to Mickie Most's famous studios at RAK in North London and Levine took the opportunity to recruit some new horn players for the songs 'Jericho' and 'Come To My Aid', which Mick had written during the recording. They sat alongside the songs the band played regularly as part of the live show, but even then Levine wanted to change things.

"'Holding Back The Years' was changed dramatically in the studio and was entirely different to the live version. I always heard it in a different way to the way Mick had been doing it and we spent the whole day in the studio – never came out at all – making that track," explains Levine.

The new in-studio combination of Mick and Levine was proving a hit. "He was fantastic on the album, wide open to all and everything I suggested" is Levine's abiding memory of *Picture Book*. "I never had to compromise and he understood when I had a problem with people in his band and that was also when he learnt the art of using a microphone in a recording studio."

Despite the fact that he had watched and learned as visiting musicians worked wonders with a mike on stage in Manchester's clubland, Mick had still to perfect the art in the studio and Levine was the man to teach him. "I taught him that the microphone is your friend, you have to keep your feet pivoted and move your head. He was fascinated and went from being unrecordable on the first couple of days to becoming by far the best singer I have ever known on a microphone."

High praise indeed from a man who played saxophone on Little Eva's classic hit 'The Locomotion', and whose career as a producer at that time spanned over three decades. And Levine wasn't finished with the compliments. "At the end I

Band: Left to right: Fritz McIntyre, Tony Bowers,
Tim Kellett, Chris Joyce, Sylvan Richardson
and Mick

was knocked out by the album and it's still my favourite album. I love the energy on the record – it was a snapshot of the conversation I had with Mick the night we met. It was just what we had in mind to make."

"Picture Book was more of a collection of songs recorded and written over a two-to-four year period. We worked the songs out through doing concerts and Levine changed quite a lot of the ideas.

The song Picture Book was about a painting in the National Gallery – a painting that seemed to have so much faith, all the faith of the Renaissance period. I just wanted to make something that was very dramatic in that sort of heavenly sense. It was in admiration of this picture. None of the other songs have any particular concept."

If the album left Levine overjoyed, the cover artwork – photographed by Simon Fowler and designed by Peter Barrett – made a less favourable impression on Reg Hucknall. "I never liked that image on the cover – it made him look like that Irish singer Gilbert O'Sullivan. It used to remind me of him with that daft hat on."

"I like the cover photo. All the band had their photos done but it was Elliot's decision to have me on the cover and I went along with it. Initially I would have been quite happy to have had a group photograph on the front but I was persuaded not just by Elliot, but also by Simon Potts at Elektra. This was at the start of our relationship with the label and in any relationship there is a little bit of give-and-take."

Among those waiting expectantly to listen to the brand new first album from Simply Red was journalist Adrian Thrills who was keen to compare the band he saw live with what came out of the studio. Despite Levine's misgivings and studio tinkering, Thrills was converted. "They were a really tight band and his voice was extraordinary. They captured the excitement of songs of a young band as they were played live and you can't really ask for any more of a debut album."

"On hearing Picture Book at that time the majority of the band weren't satisfied with the sound and I felt the same way. Part of it was because the band wanted a sound that they couldn't get – which Stewart knew – but they couldn't understand that. Me and Tony Bowers, because we were such lovers of dub reggae, were trying to get more bass on the record but it was the wrong way of doing it, and I know now that the bass has to be controlled.

The album as an entity is about that moment in time. I can't play it now, I sound like I'm about seven years old and the sound of the instrumentation is quite thin and tinny and very much of the 1980s with a huge banging snare drum. Some tracks still work like, 'Sad Old Red', but I know we've got better versions of the songs now through live or new studio recordings."

Even though he avoided the urge to go off and explore new musical influences at this early stage of his career, Mick's performance, according to

Thrills, still caused some people to ask questions. "It went right back to that old thing about can white men sing the blues? The fact is that here was a white guy from Manchester doing essentially music of black origin, and for some people that caused its own little debate."

Thrills, however, was confident that, as time went by, Mick would want to branch out and stretch himself musically with each new album. "He's got a good knowledge of music and knows a lot about the history of music. If he hears something going on somewhere he'll investigate it and maybe pick up on it, and perhaps integrate it into his own music."

The chance to experiment with new ideas arrived with the band's second album *Men And Women*, recorded between dates on the 1986 world tour.

While the band remained the same, Mick chose a new producer to bring things together, and the band's add-on saxophone player Ian Kirkham thinks he knows why there was a change. "The change to Alex Sadkin was, I think, because Mick wanted a more live, raw sound, a bit like the Ohio Players, than the wider sounds of the first album."

According to Dodd, Mick and Simply Red might just have fallen foul of the music industry's notorious reputation concerning second albums, particularly those that follow a hit. "As with all bands the recording process for the second album perhaps came too soon." That said, Dodd is a fan of the *Men And Women* album and one track in particular. "Ironically the monitor mixes sounded infinitely better than the final release and Love Fire has got to be one of Mick's best performances. I always regret that it wasn't a single."

He also understands the thinking behind Sadkin being chosen as producer explaining simply that Mick had been thrust on to the world stage, tried one producer and was anxious to see who and what else was out there. Sadly it didn't work out to be the perfect marriage of artist and producer as Dodd recounts. "Sadkin was more of a current pop producer and Mick's roots lay somewhat deeper than that and he was also divisive between Mick and the band. But the engineer Barry Mraz, who had worked with the Ohio Players, was fantastic although tragically he had a terminal illness and was dead within six months – and then Alex died tragically as well."

The people at WEA, who were now responsible for Simply Red's releases, recognised Sadkin's credentials. "He was hot at the time," says Max Hole. "But having said that, I don't think he ever got to grips with Mick who, by then, sort of thought he knew how to produce a record."

"Simon Potts suggested Alex Sadkin again for Men And Women and I just wanted to work with another producer because after my first album, I wanted to go out into the big wide world and see what else was out there and experience working with other people. I liked very much his work with Grace Jones and James Brown

and with Sly and Robbie. There was some dissatisfaction in the band about the sound on Picture Book, *the final mix disturbed us and I told Stewart that I wanted to work with somebody else and test the water to see what else was out there. That was the only intention.*

Obviously Stewart wasn't happy about me using Alex. He had done some amazing work as a producer but right from the beginning, from the first time I met Stewart, I told him that I wanted to do what he did, that I was going to learn from him. I became his sidekick in the band. I'd written the songs so I wanted to be involved. I was very open about it."

Levine, the man who lost out as producer, puts his non-appearance on the follow-up album down to an argument he had with Mick at a party thrown by the producer at his house in London. "We were both drunk and disagreed about something – it could have been reggae. Either way, we had a big fist fight out in the backyard and somehow things were never right again after that," is Levine's recollection of what went on. But he accepts it might not be the only reason, "I think the fight precipitated the move but Mick might see it differently."

The two of them had also discussed – and disagreed over – the collection of songs Mick wanted to include on the new album. "He played them to me and I thought they weren't up to the level of what he needed and I let it be known. We did agree to disagree and I didn't feel I could make as a good an album the second time round."

Even then, Mick's decision to opt for Sadkin left Levine less than ecstatic. "I wasn't happy about him moving on but it happened. I'm a New York Bronx boy and he's a tough kid from Manchester and neither of us take no shit from anyone. Actually that was part of why we got on in the first place."

"I met with Sadkin and told him I wanted to co-produce with him. I would have appreciated it if he said something like, 'I wouldn't want to do it as equals, I think you should assistant produce or something like that' but what he said was, 'Let's see at the end of the album.' Like a naive idiot I believed him and agreed to that.

I didn't know then that Alex had a little bit of a bullying streak in him and he spent the entire time slowly but surely undermining my views and opinions and taking sides with different members of the band. It was about keeping me in my place.

It's a shame to say it now because he's passed away but that was the true situation and it was the closest I came to actually quitting. Halfway through the album, I called my then American manager and said, 'I don't want to do this anymore, if this is making music then I don't want to do it.'"

As *Men And Women* began to take shape, it became clear, as Hole recalls, that the Hucknall/Sadkin partnership wasn't working perfectly. "Sadkin turned out to be more of a recording engineer than a producer which was not what we had in mind."

There was, however, better news with the choice of the first single. "There was a small team working on everything to do with Simply Red. It was Mick, Elliot

Rashman, Rob Dickins and me and we were all in favour of 'The Right Thing,'" says Hole.

Hole and Dickins were from the school that believed an act should go with the strongest single first and were perhaps proved right with a number 11 hit, although the follow-up disappointed two of the team. "Certainly Mick and Elliot thought 'Infidelity' would be bigger than it was and after that persuading Mick to release 'Ev'ry Time We Say Goodbye' as a single was a struggle," adds Hole, "but Elliot was on our side with that one."

The Cole Porter classic, while it represented Mick's accredited debut as a producer (albeit as co-producer with Yvonne Ellis), was a track that was not even scheduled to be on the album, let alone released as a single. "Mick argued that it was like a demo," admits Hole, "which in a way it was, because it was originally recorded as a bonus track or as a B-side. But that was partly my role, to persuade Mick to do singles he didn't want to do or include tracks on albums and often, I was in cahoots with Elliot. Sometimes Elliot would think it might be better if I tried to persuade Mick, and at other times we'd work it vice versa."

"'The Right Thing' got banned and there was a little inverted racism in it. If I was a black guy I would have got away with it because R&B has much more basic lyrics – ask someone like Millie Jackson – and the innuendo in Afro-American music is all over the place. We got banned but I really didn't give two hoots.
I'll go along with Max if he says that I needed persuading for 'Ev'ry Time We Say Goodbye' to be a single but if you asked me now I'd say it was definitely a single. 'Infidelity' was all about an article in Melody Maker *that started off about my libido and my reaction, because I got criticised, was to lash out as opposed to playing a smarter game. It was the first time I worked with Lamont Dozier which was great because he is a legend, a hero, and I had all the Motown singles. I had to keep slowing him down because as an ideas machine he is unstoppable. He'd try one idea, then another melody would follow another idea and the next melody would follow that."*

Record exec Hole's final contribution to *Men And Women* was to insist on a change of album sleeve. "The original cover was something terrible and didn't have Mick on the front which we thought was pretty ridiculous."

"The cover of Men And Women *was an 'If it ain't broke then don't fix it' routine. Most of the band weren't happy about it even though we had success with the first album with just me on the front cover. I wasn't overly happy about it either and had conversations with my management on virtually every record about diverting the attention off me. I didn't think it was fair that it should be me all the time because I was taking all the fucking heat."*

One of the first outsiders to hear the new album was Thrills, who saw the band's debut album as a strong reflection of their strength as a live act, but the follow-up left him with some doubts. "With second albums you sometimes have to seek new inspiration and I don't know if Mick found that or not with *Men And Women*".

"If there's any album I want to get hold of and re-mix it's Men And Women. *It was there on the tape. We heard it and people like Rob Dickins and Max Hole loved it; it sounded very natural, just like the band but then it came to the final mixes and it was like banana-republic politics. The album got ruined in the mixes. At one point Alex had three engineers in three different studios working on the same track – and all at our expense."*

As the band moved on to their third album, so Hole's role took on a new importance in the Simply Red organisation. "I became part of the inner circle around that time. Up to that point all the decisions came from them but, by now I was pretty close with Mick and was also tight with Elliot."

While Hole rightly took some credit for helping to bring Levine back into the fold, the producer himself was somewhat reluctant to return to the scene. "I was surprised when they asked me and I wasn't sure I wanted to do it," says Levine. "Max said Mick wanted me to do it and I had met Mick at a show in New York after the second album and we had a good time talking about music."

"Back to Stewart for A New Flame *because it was a winning combination and I'd had my experience elsewhere, thank you very much. I think you learn more when things go wrong than when they go right and I'd never had a problem with Stewart. When I came back to working with him I was happy and our relationship was the same, if not even better."*

If that conversation was the catalyst for Mick deciding that working with Levine again was the right move, things didn't seem quite so perfect to Levine. "It wasn't easy, they were difficult times for Mick and the band and it was all a bit uncomfortable," was his initial reaction, and when he heard what was planned for the record he had further reservations. "I was not thrilled with the material when I first heard it but we worked hard at adding to it. Mick worked with Lamont Dozier and Joe Sample and that all worked out too."

Following the departure of guitarist Sylvan, Levine dipped into his contact book again and invited Brazilian guitarist Heitor T.P. to join the band for the recording sessions at George Martin's AIR Studios in Monserrat.

"After Sylvan left, Stewart found Heitor and I liked him immediately. He played in a beautiful Brazilian way – floral and melodic, which floated – and while the digging into the rhythm was not as much in his nature, he could play R&B as well. The whole band was now getting more sophisticated with our playing ability."

If Heitor, who actually replaced Aziz Ibrahim who had toured with the band but never appeared on an album, was pleased to be joining the band – "he was

THE RIGHT THINGE   (HUCKNALL)   © SO WHAT MUSIC LTD
1986

① In the middle of the night, when the time is right

Sexily right I'm gonna do the right thing.

Gonna move you slow, much harder though

Sexily so, I'm gonna do the right thing.

Feelin hot, I ain't never gonna stop

To get what you got, you'd better take what I bring

● Feel it now much Harder now

More than any old how, say you feel the Pain.

✱ Feel I'm getting harder now, get off your back Four

  GET ON TOP MORE.
Feel I'm sinking farther down, get off your back Four

  GET ON TOP MORE   OWWWW ♪

② I told you to stop, "You're sleeping out a lot"

● You told me get lost, where's your understanding

I feel it now much harder than I've ever done now

  I'd better do the right thing.

(chorus) I'm gonna do the right thinge.

✱
        REPEAT 1st Verse   chorus
Chorus +
REFRAIN   I'm on fire (rpt)

You know I told you that I would never dream of leaving

if I did it right (rpt)

I'm gonna do the right THINGE ♪

blown away" according to Levine – back at WEA UK, Hole was even more delighted that Levine was back behind the desk.

"The brilliant thing about Stewart was that he had enough gravitas and experience that in a clever way he could tell Mick where to get off. Mick was always impatient in the studio and Stewart was good at slowing him down," explains Hole, adding, "and he was also good at recording good performances and telling Mick that they weren't good enough."

Levine also had to resist Mick's new-found enthusiasm for production and his desire to be involved behind both the mixing desk and the microphone. "It was an area that he was fascinated by and he showed some interest in but I didn't want to go that route at that particular time, so I turned down the idea of Mick being co-producer or associate producer or whatever on that album."

As the sessions for *A New Flame* began on the Caribbean island, Kirkham – now a fully fledged band member – began to notice the first signs of friction and it was all about songs and songwriting. "We were doing some B-sides and Mick was saying, 'You guys do something you want to do and we'll put it on the B-side,' but then there was an argument about the royalty payments."

The recording progressed but people in the band stopped talking to each other and began to split into various small camps. For Kirkham, this represented the beginnings of a major rift in the group. "I wasn't privy to a lot of what was going on but I remember that Tim Kellett and Tony Bowers weren't getting on and when Fritz and Mick were playing pool – they're both quite competitive – it was all going off there as well."

Recording in Monserrat was Levine's idea, based on the fact that the band were already tax exiles living in Italy. "I had made an album there and thought it would be a good place to go – somewhere where a bunch of Mancunians could get some warm weather." But it wasn't long before the producer realised that his best-laid plans were not working. "There was tension between Mick and Tony and between Fritz and Mick but we got over it and sometimes you can use that tension to make a record work."

In late 1988 Levine delivered the third Simply Red album and despite the problems, the tension and the warring camps, he was full of optimism for the record. "I think the album put him right back up there although I didn't think it had quite the vitality and energy of *Picture Book*."

"I don't actually remember it being our first number one album – we'd been on a train of work all the time and missed that bit of news. But reality came back with this record and I still criticise the record company in a way because I do think they could have sold more albums than they did. We were always an albums band but now were being seen as this pop band who had hit singles. It was bizarre."

Gold Award for *A New Flame*, left to right:
Tim Kellett, Andy Dodd, Tony Bowers,
Stewart Levine, Chris Joyce, Mick,
Fritz McIntyre and Elliot Rashman

Back in London, the decision about the first single from the new album rested – as usual – with Mick, Rashman and Hole and they went for 'It's Only Love' but a new version that would, in turn, lead to more friction in the Simply Red set-up.

"I had a remix done of 'It's Only Love' because the rhythm section was a bit lumpy" admits Hole. "Stewart Levine was really angry about it but Mick, Elliot and I all thought it was great, so we went with it as the single but not on the album."

The top twenty hit helped take the new album to number one just as the follow-up single was being debated and this time, according to Hole, it was the singer who had his doubts. "Mick did not want to go with 'If You Don't Know Me By Now' because he really didn't want consecutive covers as the first two singles. He always wanted 'A New Flame' but again Elliot and I conspired and managed to persuade him."

Up to this stage, Simply Red had continued with their tried and tested philosophy of releasing an album every two years and touring pretty much non-stop between each album. But early in 1990, after three albums and almost five years of constant globe-trotting, Mick took his band off the road for over a year in order to rest, write and plan the next move.

The lead-up to album number four saw the departure of original band members Bowers and Joyce and the recruitment of programmer and drummer Gota alongside bass player Shaun Ward, but once again Levine was at the helm, although he sensed a new enthusiasm on Mick's part.

"Gota coming in changed the sound and coincided with me spending more time in London and becoming fascinated with that programming sound. All the Madchester stuff had kicked off in the Hacienda and there was all this Ecstasy around and this other kind of synthetic beat.

I wanted something that sounded more organic and humane instead of just raw electro. This was my quest for the next two or three albums – crossing the bridges between electronic music and played music so that you got the sort of sound that Massive Attack and Soul II Soul had. I wanted to be influenced by it but also formulate stuff that was played as music.

Looking back, if I had my way now, I would have stuck with real instrumentation and not done it that other way – but that's all in retrospect."

"We started to do some demos for the new album which were quite good but I wanted to make sure we were better prepared. Mick made some good working demos and then there was the request that he be involved in the production," says Levine, who agreed that the time was right. "I thought, 'Well alright, he's contributed,' so I didn't have an issue with a co-producer credit."

"I co-produced Stars *with Stewart. I had made a big contribution to* A New Flame *but Stewart definitely made a bigger contribution. But now I wanted to work some more machinery as well as the songs and I just negotiated for it because I had an idea of the direction I wanted to go with* Stars.

The demos I made in Manchester are certainly not dissimilar to the finished version and what Stewart did was keep the human side in the playing. It was very much working together, very harmonious and we had a good relationship all the way through."

After abandoning the original studios in Paris, the new seven-piece line-up travelled to the Condulmer studios in Venice to make the album that was to seal the name Simply Red in the history of popular music. For Kirkham, *Stars* represented something special even as the band started to lay down the first tracks.

"It seemed to me that there were songs here that were potentially very successful pop records and were different to the soul thing we had done in the past. There was definitely a sense of Mick having something to prove, he was a man on a mission with *Stars*."

Possibly Mick's most significant contribution to the *Stars* album were the ten songs he wrote. For the first time, a Simply Red album contained no cover versions and no songs composed by other writers. Even though there were two compositions co-written with McIntyre it was essentially all Mick, and Levine openly acknowledges the quality of the compositions. "He wrote ten great songs and that was a major achievement."

"With the hits on A New Flame coming from 'It's Only Love' and 'If You Don't Know Me By Now' it was fair criticism to say, 'What about some original songs,' although we did have a hit with the title track which was a big song for me. But I was determined to write the songs on Stars.

Getting ribbed about songwriting spurred me on and basically I wrote all those songs to prove something, mostly to myself but also to the people who criticised me over the cover versions."

Again, Thrills was there to offer a critic's view of the finished work. "It was one of those albums where the whole was greater than the sum of the parts. What you hear is Mick's voice, the songs, some fantastic hooks and melodies and some heartfelt lyrics and the whole things just hangs together."

"Some of the songs were formulated during the tour before we started recording. 'Something Got Me Started' and 'Stars' I did while we were on the road. 'Thrill Me' is one of the songs where Fritz came up with the riff which was the first spark and we just worked on it on stage. I love the track 'How Could I Fall' because I like music playing on my records and I like other people solo-ing on my records and 'How Could I Fall' has that quality. I'm not making a single here: it's about something I want to listen to as a piece of ethereal music and just get off on the musicians playing and the arrangement."

The album also represented a move forward for the members of the band, as Kirkham explains. "We just wanted to make a really good-sounding record

and it did sound different because Gota's programming made it different. I remember that the Soul II Soul stuff really hit Mick hard and he wanted that sort of cool sound about the record."

Another major factor in the success of *Stars* was undoubtedly the concept for the design of the album sleeve and after her initial press photo shoot Zanna was booked to come up with a brief.

Her first idea centred around a 1920s movie image of a film actress with stars falling out of the sky. Her reference photo linked in with Mick's ideas for an album called *Stars* and quickly became the theme for the design of the album cover.

Mick brought another element to the visual mix with his plan to wear a magnificent painted cloak he had bought in Spain. "We had other options for clothes but Mick just wanted to wear the cloak and have his legs bare – he'd got great legs so it wasn't a problem," explains Zanna.

Before embarking on the shoot with Mick, Zanna tested the set-up by photographing her assistant in exactly the right pose, which also meant that she would not be testing Mick's patience.

"We had this attention-span issue with Mick and I didn't think I'd have very long, so I just got on and took the shot," she recalls. "Then there was some umming and aahing about whether he ought to have trousers on or not. Mick was adamant that he wanted to wear the cloak with bare legs and look natural, realistic."

With this shot proposed as the cover design, East West did some research and back came the answer that Mick should indeed be wearing trousers. It was in fact East West in America who were most concerned with Mick's lack of trousers because, as Dodd recalls, "Sylvia Rhone's research showed that the bare legs looked 'too gay' for America." But without a single photo of Mick wearing trousers, Zanna struggled for an answer which wouldn't involve bringing Mick back for another session.

"Then I remembered the lighting test I'd done with my assistant. I had one roll of film with her and she had jeans on." Even then, Zanna faced the problem of fitting the jeans onto Mick's legs. "We used one of the first digital re-touching computers and I'm sure we spent a lot of money forming the jeans to fit his legs."

"The cover with no trousers was hilarious. There was this thought in America that it looked too feminine so we put the jeans on afterwards. It was an example of a record company getting it right. I bought the cloak that's on the back cover in Spain but it came from Mexico and I just thought it might be great for covering my head between shoots in the desert – and I was right, because it was too damn hot in the Californian desert."

The finished artwork – with Mick sporting a pair of lady's legs and his Native American cloak – worked on different levels for Zanna. "There is a sort of Bob Marley quality there. He was perhaps trying to span a number of cultures in one image and I think he achieved that, and perhaps that's why it was hugely successful."

Having delivered the album – and the artwork – to his own and his record company's satisfaction, it was back on the road for Mick and Simply Red, with two years of worldwide touring while East West continued their campaign, stretching it into a remarkable three years.

For Kirkham and the rest of the band, *Stars* also represented a unique moment in time. "*Stars* was like a blip in time when everything came together on a completely different level."

"We never thought it was going to be that big but every time you're trying to better the last album, and when we finished we knew it was something that was very strong. Sergeant Pepper is one of those records that is a concept in its entirety more than any of the other albums The Beatles made, and that's what Stars was. This sort of organic concept in its own entirety."

For all of 1994 and most of 1995, Simply Red took time out to recover from the gruelling non-stop campaign that kept *Stars* among the best-selling albums of all-time and saw it confirmed as going 30 times platinum across Europe.

As a result, the gap between Simply Red albums stretched to four years and unfortunately the return to the studio to make *Life* was not the happy experience everybody hoped for.

"Stars and Life are very much musing on this understanding of the organics of it all. We got here because maybe something out there hit this place and brought the water that made all this happen. I began to believe in things like an energy force, that energy is what it's all about and then you have this kind of humility about your own consciousness because I'm just a bit of this energy that's floating around the universe, and I just happened to be at this particular time. From the Big Bang theory and everything like that, it just occurred to me that we are all made out of star dust."

"*Life* was not fun to make," is how Levine sums it up. "I never bought into the concept that *Stars* was a hard album to follow. It's easy to follow a ten million seller, what's hard is following a record that sold just ten thousand. But it was a difficult record to make because there was no joy around it. Mick was very much into wanting to control things and I did not have a good time on it," explains Levine who also disagreed with Mick's move towards hip hop music. "I didn't think he had to worry about being trendy, he had this fantastic voice and that's what put him there, but he wanted to be part of what was happening at the time."

Simply Red
life

Even the people at East West noticed that all was not well in the Simply Red camp. "Making the record was troublesome," confirms Hole. "There were problems between Mick and Stewart as they kept falling out, but Mick was always confident about his music. I don't know whether he had doubts late at night but I never saw any self-doubt."

"It was our third number one album in a row but it would be tough for anyone to follow the success of Stars. *We had four hit singles but it didn't translate into album sales in the same way and in some ways you could argue that it was inevitable."*

With Gota gone along with bassist Shaun Ward and keyboard/trumpet player Tim Kellett, Simply Red was now reduced to a basic three-piece – McIntyre, Kirkham and Heitor – behind Mick, with celebrated musicians such as Sly Dunbar, Robbie Shakespeare, Bootsy Collins, Ritchie Stevens, Danny Cummings and Hugh Masekela all lending a hand.

Even then, the sessions in Manchester's Planet 4 Studios, Air Studios in London and Downtown Studios in Johannesburg left a lasting impression on Kirkham, who was working on his fourth album. "*Life* was the toughest album for everyone. People were falling out and Stewart wasn't involved at the start. Maybe Mick wanted to do the production himself after *Stars*. But it still went quite smoothly because it was never rushed."

The tension in the studio reached such a level that managers Dodd and Rashman were called in to rescue the situation. "Stewart had a very tough time during *Life* and at one point Elliot and I had to go down and persuade him not to leave the project," says Dodd, who put it down to "Mick growing as an artist and clearly wanting more control over things, it is part of the evolution of most artists."

"After Stars, Life *was intended to be my masterpiece – I wanted to have two masterpieces and I still think it's a very strong album. If I was going to criticise myself about* Life *it's that there should have been more co-writes on it. I should have expanded my menu at that point and worked with other writers. I wasn't doing it with Fritz – he went on a go-slow – so the whole thing is too static. The music around the songs and the writing is a little bit slow and a little bit lazy."*

While Mick and Stewart shared the production credit on *Life*, a new name now appeared on the cast list. Andy Wright was hired to fill the programming role previously occupied by Gota and his work started before the recording sessions began. "Most of the initial work was done between myself, Mick, Ian Kirkham and the engineer Roland Herrington. This was two or three months before Stewart Levine came in, and I think Andy and Elliot were keen for Stewart to be there to keep a hand on Mick in the studio."

Sadly it didn't quite work out that way and even newcomer Wright was dragged into the situation. "I think Mick decided he wanted to do it himself, so it was

Side 1

1. You Make Me Believe — 3.51
2. So Many People — 5.19
3. Lives And Loves — 3.21
4. Fairground — 5.33
5. Never Never Love — 4.19

Side 2

1. So Beautiful — 4.58
2. Hillside Avenue — 4.45
3. Remembering The First Time — 4.43
4. Out On The Range — 6.00
5. We're In This Together — 4.14

0630-12069-1 France CA651 A Time Warner Company

all a bit of political struggle and to some degree I ended up in the middle. If making the record was the only issue in the studio it would have been really easy but when there are agendas and politics, it's less than perfect."

According to Wright, his relationship with Mick got off to a good start. "We got on to a good wavelength straight away. He pretty well knew what he wanted and I could deliver it at pretty high speed. At the end of the first day he shook my hand and said it had been a pleasure working with me – and first impressions are always important."

'Fairground' was the song that gave Mick and Simply Red their first ever UK number one hit single and it was also the first chart-topper Wright had worked on. "Mick said he had this idea for a carnival-style track we were doing the next day. I don't think he actually had the song, I think he wrote it that night. That's my take on it, and it's a great compliment to him that he could write a song like that overnight."

"Quite a few of the songs have survived, that's what I like about Life. *'Fairground' being number one was fantastic – it was the first thing I worked on with Andy Wright. There are so many tracks that we still perform live like 'You Make Me Believe', 'Fairground', 'Never Never' and 'So Beautiful' which was the single that never was. I think that should have been a single and I think it would have been a hit but we'd had so many bloody singles before it that everybody just gave up. Elliot and I were both tired, probably too tired to argue about it."*

The job of creating the carnival beat fell to Wright and he remembered a track he'd seen on *Top of the Pops* a month earlier. He sent out for a copy of The Goodmen's 'Give It Up' and played it to Mick. "He wasn't keen on the idea to start with but when he heard it he said, 'That's it, that's exactly it,' so we sampled it off the record, re-edited all the beats and added a Hammond organ sound that Heitor played on his guitar."

After four or five hours in the studio, a number one record was created, but even then its success surprised Kirkham. "I understand why people get 'Fairground' but I would never have had it down as a number one. Everybody was happy about it being number one but with Simply Red the focus was always on the albums."

For Dodd, the number one record that emerged out of all the troubled times in the studio, remains very special. "'Fairground' was a beautiful, evocative song. The rhythm track locked in a new generation of fans and it still remains Mick's most successful single to date."

After her creative work on *Stars*, Zanna was again retained to come up with a design to go with the album title *Life*. "The first concept for *Life* was much bigger and was going to be an art installation in a gallery." Her idea involved using the Royal Horticultural Society building as the location for a 60-foot

Zanna

high creation of the word *Life* which would be installed and opened up to the public.

With Mick's support, plans were under way to create the four letters out of rubber when the plug was pulled. "We had to order the letters six weeks in advance and we were all ready to go," says Zanna, "when the record company decided they weren't going to spend the money."

Finding herself in the middle of a stand-off between the artist and his record company, Zanna began to think of new ideas until Mick came to the rescue. "He said he was going to pay for it anyway, and they could buy it back from him."

"What I like about the cover is that I wanted it to be seen as me strolling through life – that's how I feel about it. I'm just getting on with my work, I do my job, I love my writing, I love singing and I'm just getting on with my life."

The change in style and the new partnership with programming expert Wright had an impact on Adrian Thrills who was now working as a sports writer and listening to Simply Red for pleasure. "That Euro-house sound on 'Fairground' was very much adapted to his own songwriting. He picked up on things, not just historical influences, and incorporated modern contemporary sounds into a traditional soul format."

While *Life* may have been another chart-topping album for Simply Red which earned them their greatest ever single success, it also signalled the end of an enormously successful period for Levine as the band's producer.

"After this, Stewart Levine had nothing more to offer me. I thought he'd run out of ideas and maybe I wasn't listening to any ideas – maybe it was a mixture of both. It was just the coming to the end of a cycle and I look at it as no more than that."

"Mick had become an even more forceful character," is how Levine sums it all up. "He really wanted to be a producer which always made me laugh because if I could sing like him I wouldn't bother with producing. But he got fascinated by production and then he lost the plot – you can't do it all, nobody ever has."

Then, as if to disprove Levine's assertion that he wanted to 'do it all', Mick assembled a new team to produce the next Simply Red album. *Blue* saw Mick continue his relationship with Wright and also welcome Gota back into the fold and – as AGM – the three of them set about recording in London, Kingston and New York.

Even though he was in part stepping into Levine's shoes, Wright did understand what the American producer was saying. "Mick would make a great producer for someone else, but when he's making his own albums he does need an outside perspective."

Painting by Mick for the *Blue* release

Initially neither Wright nor Gota were asked to work as producers, but as they heard what Mick had in mind for his new album, they gradually became more and more involved. "When Mick played me some songs I thought I could do some arrangements over and above drumming and programming," recalls Gota. "So I gave him a few of my ideas and he asked me to help with the production."

For Wright, it started with Mick's plan to do an entire album of cover versions and being sent a cassette of 'The Air That I Breathe'. "I wasn't really interested in just being a programmer and after I did a version of 'The Air That I Breathe' he called me up and asked if I wanted to co-produce with him and Gota. After that," says Wright, "he basically gave me and Gota the tracks and gave us free rein to come up with ideas."

"There are some nice moments on the album. I think the experimentation is nice. It was the first time I was going into Andy Wright territory a lot more – the marriage of machines and playing and sampling. I thought it was time to experiment. I was trying to find a new sound. I thought Andy's techno-y, sample-y work married with Gota's organic approach to machinery would make a good blend together. I didn't really produce these tracks in the same way as I produced with Stewart. I basically gave them the songs and they went off to their studios and worked on them.

I started out with me trying to do virtually a covers album and I spent a lot of money and a lot of time and I shouldn't have been doing it. It was all a waste of time and a very expensive waste of time on my part. We clawed it back by bringing in Andy and Gota and making something worthwhile. I think there are some good moments on Blue.*"*

Wright, whose production credits include Jeff Beck, Luciano Pavarotti, Atomic Kitten, S Club 7 and Natalie Imbruglia, recognised two stand-out tracks on *Blue*. "On 'Some Day In My Life' I got David Whittaker to do a string arrangement and had Mick sing in the studio with the full orchestra. It was a great moment. But for me 'Love Has Said Goodbye Again' was the track which, if we'd got it right, would have been the smash hit from the album. And we nearly got it right at one point but then it just got away from us," explains Wright. "Mick loves making records but he does get a bit bored at times."

While Mick, Kirkham, Gota, backing singer Dee Johnson and session bass player Sly Dunbar were the only musicians from *Life* to appear on *Blue*, there were a total of 18 new musicians and for some – Sarah Brown, John Johnson, Steve Lewinson, Kenji Suzuki and Mark Jaimes – it was to be the passport into what was slowly emerging as the new Simply Red.

Throughout his career Mick has regularly covered classic songs and put his own stamp on them, but musicians and producers know that it is an area fraught with danger. While a cover of a Led Zeppelin track never made it on to the final version of the *Blue* album, Wright still had his reservations about Mick's version of a 1970s classic that gave him a number six hit in 1998.

"I wasn't entirely keen on 'The Air That I Breathe' but because of The Hollies it was a Manchester song and I believe that was the thinking behind covering it," says Wright, who admits that at that early stage in his relationship with Mick he didn't feel confident about airing his views too strongly. "Now, if there were songs I didn't think were right I'd say so and probably wouldn't agree to take them on."

"Another person's song is a challenge and I try to choose songs that I can do a sublime version of. I don't work on a ratio of covers to my own songs and I'll have a list of songs in my mind and think, 'I'll do that song one day'.

Before I did it, 'It's Only Love' was on the B-side of an obscure single and no one really knew 'Money's Too Tight To Mention' until I'd done it but some people are just too good to do covers of. Otis Redding is taboo, The Beatles are very difficult because the engineering of their records is a huge inspiration to what I've been doing recently, Billie Holiday is a big danger and it's pretty silly to try and do any James Brown songs."

While Mick considers covering the legendary blues singer Billie Holiday to be "a big danger" he has impressed Jools Holland with his ability to mimic the very finest singers around. "Mick's a very good impersonator. He does a good Billie Holiday and a very good Frank Sinatra which he has done with our big band."

As one of the handful of players who retained their place in the Simply Red team, brass player Kirkham saw at first hand the ups and downs of life in the studio with Mick... and it wasn't always consistent. "Mick can be so particular about things and then not give a toss at the same time – it's strange, like his focus changes."

Making *Blue* was in fact one of the least pleasurable experiences in Kirkham's time with the band. As the sessions stretched on and on, he got a sense that some of his fellow musicians were not right for the job. "It took so long and it had some of the wrong guys playing on it. It wasn't any more complicated but there didn't seem to be a focus." is how he sums it up before adding, "It was like – here's a song, let's just play it – and if you have the wrong guys playing it ends up sounding like a jam session. I think Elliot said it sounded like the David Letterman band."

"It was exactly what it said on the tin – blue! In a strange way these were the hard times with a lot of mental challenges for me to deal with. I was on a slight self-destruct thing but also wanted to carry on. I'd lost Heitor, I'd lost Fritz – which was inevitable – I knew I wasn't going to work with Stewart Levine for a while and Elliot quit. I'd also blown a relationship in my personal life that I shouldn't have blown.

I decided to go through the cathartic artist routine – if I'm blue then I'm gonna show it and you're going to get some of it. Not only was it cathartic for me but maybe it would be for any of the listeners who were going through the same sort

SIMPLY RED
BLUE

of thing. There is a case for sharing it – it's good to show the bad times as well as the good times in a long-term career."

Blue also marked the final appearance on a Simply Red album cover shoot for photographer Zanna whose role initially was to photograph one of Mick's paintings that he had designated as the front cover artwork.

She remembers well the constant to-ing and fro-ing that went on between her and Mick. "It was a painting of a piano, and it was delivered to my studio for me to photograph. Then Mick wanted to add to it, so it went back and forth a couple more times before I finally got it back for the picture to be taken."

With the picture lying on her studio floor, Zanna worked out how to hang it and light it to get the best effect and, when she finally took a test Polaroid, she spotted a mark on the painting. "We took it down and, noticed there was a cat's paw print on the painting. Then I realised that, when I finally got it back from Mick, the paint hadn't dried and my cat had walked right across the wet painting."

"My painting was intended for the cover but Zanna's photograph won me over. I liked the work Zanna did with us. She did good work and was very passionate about things despite me being a pain in the arse. I didn't always get my own way on these things and tried to see it as what's the best way to get the thing right."

Eventually – and consistently – East West made the decision that the front cover should be a photo of Mick so the painting was re-assigned to the back cover while the original was returned to Mick – complete with the cat's paw print. "I never told Mick and it's probably still there today," says Zanna, who also admits that her last task as Mick's photographer was to turn his eyes blue in the chosen cover shot. "I don't think it was the right thing to do but you make wrong decisions some times and that was how it ended up. Some people said he looked a bit scary."

Even though *Blue* signalled the end of her working relationship with Mick, Zanna believes that he was a person who profited from retaining relationships with people he trusted. "If he felt comfortable he was willing to be generous and share his success and say, 'Let's do it again.' Both he and Elliot liked the comfort factor and didn't really want to change things after every album."

"He needs to be stimulated because sitting in front of a camera for a long time is hard for anyone but the point was that Mick's album covers were conceptual and usually worked better with just him rather than a conglomeration of the different individuals who make up the band."

With her work appearing on three studio albums and two Simply Red collections, Zanna's contribution to the success of the band has never been overlooked by those closest to the heart of Simply Red. "She's been extremely influential in the history of the band," says Dodd, "and in defining the public image of Mick Hucknall. She's a phenomenal photographer and her work with Elliot on the *Life* campaign was nothing less than genius."

Returning to the world of music after nearly ten years away, Adrian Thrills was overwhelmed with what he heard, despite what some of his fellow critics said about *Blue*. "It was great to come back and immediately be hit with a record from an artist I'd written about when I started on *NME*, who was still producing stuff that had a real relevance."

Acknowledging that there might be a hint of rose-coloured spectacles about his view, Thrills adds, "That's very much a personal thing. There are probably more complete Simply Red albums, but I still think it's one of his best."

As a man who regularly meets and interviews Hucknall, Thrills has also had the opportunity to discuss and debate the music and records of Simply Red with the band's main man on more than one occasion. "Even though he is regularly revising his opinion of his own records, Mick did tell me that he wasn't entirely happy with either *Life* or *Blue*. For me – along with *Love And The Russian Winter* – they were part of the fall-out from *Stars* when he got into programming and using contemporary sound."

As the millennium drew to a close so did Mick's contractual commitment to East West Records. Embarking on *Love And The Russian Winter* for release in the final months of 1999, Mick chose once again to share production with Wright and Gota while assembling an assortment of old and new musicians in three London studios.

Featuring ten songs written by Mick plus the top 20 cover version of 'Ain't That A Lot Of Love', *Love And The Russian Winter* was a significant album for Mick as the second millennium dawned but it meant less to his record-buying public. It peaked at number six and brought to an end a run of five consecutive UK number one albums.

Earlier in the same year Mick got a call asking if he would consider recording a duet with one of pop music's true legends. "When the idea of the *Reload* album was suggested we put out feelers to see who would be interested in doing songs with me," explains Tom Jones. "Mick was approached and he said he'd love to do it. I was glad because I feel that he loves the same kind of music as me. Soul music is the common denominator between us."

With Mick on board the song that the pairing of Hucknall & Jones would sing came from Jones' son and manager Mark, according to the Welsh singer. "We listened to a lot of stuff and Mark asked Mick if he liked Sam and Dave songs. We agreed not to do something that had been done to death, so we sent over 'Ain't That A Lot Of Love'."

Getting together in the studio was the first time the new duo worked together and it resulted in different versions of the same song. "We did two versions

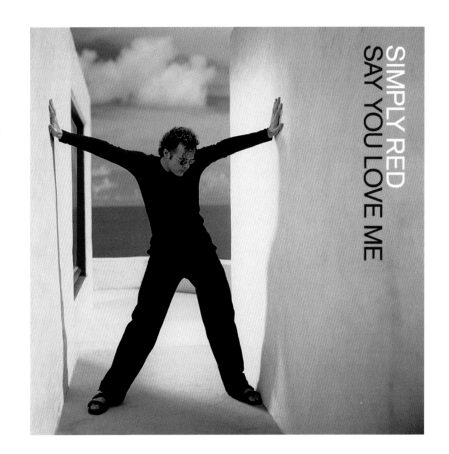

SIMPLY RED
SAY YOU LOVE ME

because Mick said he liked the song so much. They had different treatments and I had one for *Reload* and Mick had the other for his album," recalls Jones, whose career was re-launched by the million-selling chart-topping album.

Meanwhile Mick and Simply Red's version, following some in-studio work by co-producers Wright and Gota, resulted in the only top 20 hit from the last album they would make for the major label they had signed to 15 years earlier.

For Kirkham, the album represented probably his worst possible scenario as a member of Simply Red. "It was an absolute nightmare in the studio" is his simple assessment. "We only played about three tracks in a room together and those were ones that worked live; the rest of it was just synthesiser hell."

Even producer Wright had his reservations about what was going on in the studio. "It is probably Mick's least finest work – his song-writing was at the lowest point and his interest was probably pretty low too," is his honest opinion, and he doesn't excuse his own role in the proceedings.

"You have to take the blame for the albums you produce and Mick did sort of give it to us and leave us to it. Some of the ideas were slightly tired and we tried to buff them up and we didn't do that good a job of it."

"I don't think that Love And The Russian Winter *is my finest work but it shouldn't be dismissed as a contract-filler. I didn't completely neglect my work but I did basically give it to Andy and Gota and I think Andy had a lot more say over it than Gota. When I look at it now it does feel like a contract-filler but it was never intended to be and I did a lot of work on it. I don't want to disown the record completely but it was the spark for me to go back to something that sounded like Simply Red."*

Wright looks back on it now as an album that probably should never have been made. He believes Mick didn't want to make an album at that time but fulfilling his contract probably forced his hand. And it wasn't just the record that was below par, according to the new producer. "It also had the worst cover in the world and I'm vindicated in saying that because I didn't do the cover. It's all a bit of a blot on our landscape."

"The cover was my concept. It was loosely based on Dr Zhivago *and was to do with the millennium. Somebody asked me what were the two abiding things that I thought had contributed to the last century? I said love because that's eternal and the Russian winter because without that the shape of our society would have been very different when you think of Stalingrad, the Napoleonic wars and Alexander the Great."*

Both the speed and quality of the release of *Love And The Russian Winter* surprised Thrills who, even though he loved the cover version of 'Ain't That A Lot Of Love' – "it showcased Mick's voice" – was less than enthusiastic about the finished work. "It wasn't a great album and it did come out very quickly.

Top: Shooting video for 'Your Eyes'   Bottom: Mick with Tom Jones

It's unusual for an act of Mick's stature to do an album a year and it's a bit like *Blue* part two for me."

If *Love And The Russian Winter* represented something of a nadir for both band and fans alike, Wright has his own positive take on the situation. "There's something in a way quite cool about having the trough because at least people have accepted the lowest point and you can come back up again – which Mick has."

In fact, he came back up again with the release of the first album under his new simplyred.com organisation in the spring of 2003 which missed being the sixth Simply Red number one album by just a single place.

"*Home was what I would define as the sound of Simply Red and the start of a trilogy of albums where we are defining what we actually sound like. This was pretty much the first album where I used the same band for touring and on the album and it's the best Simply Red there has ever been.*

I think it's a great album but in terms of its sales performance I paid the price for not working, for not touring properly and for not being ambitious enough with Love And The Russian Winter, *but I wanted things to die down a bit.*"

Home also heralded a new recording location for Mick and Simply Red. While two tracks were done in Los Angeles and two more in London, the remaining seven were completed appropriately in Mick's new home studio and, according to Gota, who appeared as both musician and producer, it made a world of difference. "Mick was much happier and much more relaxed. He was away from record company pressures and recording at home meant he could control the time and the process. It created a more relaxed atmosphere."

In fact, before the sessions for *Home* began, Gota had helped Mick set up his new home-based studio and eased him into working behind the desk. "We set it up so he could get the sound and feel he wanted. He does want to engineer, mix and produce and I worked with him as he learnt but he's not always the easiest person to teach – he is a bit impatient."

The album saw the arrival of new drummer Pete Lewinson and the return of his brother bassist Steve Lewinson to a ten-piece line-up that was rapidly becoming the established Simply Red band.

After the disappointment of *Love And The Russian Winter*, Kirkham was anxious to put things right and recording as a band was a major step along the way for the veteran sax player. "I didn't know about him starting up his own label but when we got working it was nice to be in a room playing rather than tinkering about with technology."

"*It took two years to make because I was bouncing ideas off the musicians and learning how to use the desk when we were mixing. The roles we have in the studio are that I am the mixing engineer, Michael Zimmerling is the recording engineer*

and Andy Scade will help me with overdubs and focus on things that I miss. It took me about a year to master it and I'm still working at it but I'm really glad I've done it. I am fulfilling my potential; I am meant to do this and am getting really good at it."

With Mick acting as co-producer on all eleven tracks – along with the Lewinson brothers, Gota, Wright and Levine – Ian Kirkham was able to assess the singer's production style and skills. "He's not a hard taskmaster, but the one thing that's difficult for me with him being producer is that he knows what he wants to hear and sometimes it's not what I want to hear."

The surprise element on the new *Home* album was the return of Stewart Levine who left frustrated and disappointed after *Life* – and he accepted the return ticket reluctantly. "Andy and Ian came to me said they wanted me to work with Mick again. I wasn't that interested but they kept pestering me to try just a few songs."

Having finally agreed to do two tracks, he laid down his own ground rules for the sessions. "I said from day one that I would be the producer and Mick would be the artist – full stop!" Levine chose the Ocean Way Studios in California, picked the rhythm section he wanted – including James Gadson and Joe Sample – and agreed that all Mick would do was sing.

Close to fifteen years after he identified 'If You Don't Know Me By Now' as a song that was perfect for Mick's voice, Levine was back on the case with another soul classic and Dodd, for one, has no doubt about Levine's role in Simply Red's success. "Aside from capturing Mick's voice brilliantly, he came up with 'You Make me Feel Brand New' on which Mick displayed, at the age of 42, that he still had the vocal range of a 25-year-old.

"He also introduced Mick to Lamont Dozier and Joe Sample which expanded Mick's songwriting expertise and nobody has recorded his voice as well since," asserts Dodd.

While not disputing Levine's contribution to the sound of Mick and Simply Red on record, Jools Holland asserts that as a singer Mick is quite simply "instantly recognisable, nobody else sounds like him" and goes on to compare the singer from Manchester with one of the world's greatest-ever talents. "All the great singers have completely individual voices and that's what Mick has – he sings out of the heart. Ray Charles used to say about himself that you could like his music, you could dislike his music but when he made his music, he was completely telling the truth. And you could say the same thing about Mick Hucknall."

"*Home and Stars are my two best albums so far but there was no sense of ease about making* Home. *Ian Grenfell did a great job – he challenged me and said things could be better and as I wanted to get it right I kept at it. I enjoyed the process of writing songs with the band and it not being all my responsibility.*

SIMPLY RED
SUNRISE

We'd got seven out of ten songs completed and then Andy Wright did it again, bless him, and brought in 'Sunrise'. When we heard it we just went, 'Fucking hell, it's a hit, we've got our hit'. Then we got 'You Make Me Feel Brand New' which I did in LA with Stewart; it was great to be working with Stewart again – easy peasy."

Levine's work on the cover of the Stylistics hit song helped make Mick's new version a UK top ten hit and the third hit from *Home* but it was the first release from the album that that did most to re-establish Simply Red as a major hit band after three years out of the charts.

'Sunrise' was written by Mick and delivered to producer Wright who had already produced 'Money In My Pocket' as a potential first single. "Mick mainly did the production on *Home* himself and I just came in at the end and did the singles including 'Sunrise' which Mick had already produced a version of."

Wright's major contribution to the number seven hit was to sample the Hall & Oates 1982 hit 'I Can't Go For That (No Can Do)' and create a whole new sound picture. Why the Hall & Oates track? "I was in a record shop looking for inspiration," explains Wright, "and bought Hall & Oates and then thought that the beginning of the song would make a good sample."

From there it was back to the studio to start work combining 'Sunrise' with the Hall & Oates song. "Hall & Oates is at 110 beats per minute and 'Sunrise' is at 100 but they were in the same key so I time-stretched both of them to 105 – made their song slower and Mick's faster.

"When Mick got to the chorus which was the Hall & Oates original verse, I re-created the musical passage without them singing, dropped Mick's chorus on it and we knew from the first moment we played it back that it was a smash hit."

While Dodd has played an important part in the constant dialogue about music that has gone on over the years between artist, management, producer and record company, he recognises that currently one man has Mick's ear when it comes to commercial hits. "Andy Wright acts as a contemporary sounding board for Mick. He has one ear plugged into commercial radio and has taken most of the singles since 'Fairground' into the mainstream area."

When the new version of 'Sunrise' was delivered to publisher Peter Reichardt, who had heard Mick's original version and declared it 'OK', he immediately recognised its potential. "If ever a sample changed a record from an OK song into a major hit record, that was it."

Another man who played a role in the development and ultimate success of *Home* was string arranger and conductor Simon Hale and he did it without ever going to a recording session or even meeting Mick.

SIMPLY RED
HOME

"We spoke on the phone about three songs I was working on – 'You Make Me Feel Brand New', 'Home' and 'Sunrise' – and I was given a free hand, a blank canvas." Working with tapes delivered to his own studio, Hale set about adding strings to the music already recorded. "It's a bit like adding another chapter to a book while making it appear seamless," he explains. "But, if you took away whatever I've done, then you'd really miss it. At the same time, the listener should never realise what is going on."

With album sales close to three million and a world tour lasting nine months, Simply Red were back with a vengeance and with an energy, musical dynamism and virtuosity that didn't go unnoticed. For Adrian Thrills, this was the moment when Mick "went back to the funk and the sound of a tight band playing live in a room."

"All my favourite albums – Marvin Gaye's What's Going On*, The Beatles' albums, Rolling Stones and Led Zeppelin – are all 'played' and that's why with the* Home *album I wanted to go back to being in a room and playing the music."*

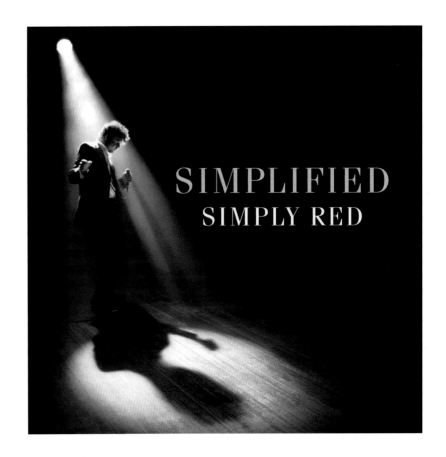

Even though his experience with Simply Red covers only three albums, Wright also believes that today's Simply Red stands out as the best band Mick has ever assembled. "It is a fabulous band. They are good to a man and a woman and good in lots of ways – they are not political and are totally supportive of Mick."

He also acknowledges that when things went wrong in the past, there were always two sides to the argument. "To be fair to some of the musicians that have come and gone, Mick is in a much better place now than he was some years ago. He is more charming, more magnanimous and more aware that he has to make an effort to keep people on his side."

Long-time manager Dodd, on hand throughout the making of *Home*, saw the process of making the album as "rewarding" and recognised the album as the most complete Simply Red album since *Stars*. "It plays as a full album and flows naturally, and it's the first album since *A New Flame* in 1989 where the band played in the same room at the same time, so it has a great feel about it."

If *Home* represented the first return on their significant investment in simplyred.com, the follow-up album *Simplified* was a musical experiment that combined old and new Simply Red with a touch of Latin music – and the first ever black-and-white Simply Red album sleeve.

Working on their second album, the design company Peacock came up with an idea based on a classic 1950s shot of a musical legend. "The cover shot is based on a shot of Frank Sinatra where he is wearing a hat and the spotlight magnifies the hat," explains Grenfell. "We'd never had a black-and-white album sleeve. Simply Red is usually all about colour but it just felt right to tie-in with *Simplified*."

Shot in Fulham Town Hall, the Simply Red album cover photograph once again features just Mick while the band are featured inside the CD booklet, and Grenfell admits that they did consider putting the whole band on the cover for the first time. "We looked at it for *Home* and on *Simplified* but having eleven band members on the cover is hard to make work as a strong image."

So, for the eleventh time a Simply Red CD went into the shops with just Mick's image on the front cover and for Dodd that has never been a problem. "As egalitarian as Mick may want to be with his band, the cover shots in my view will always be his uncluttered image. It's the purest form of marketing. You have just seconds as people scan CD racks and glance at posters so why dilute the message. And with all due respect to the public they don't give a damn about who the conga player is, they want Mick and we're here to sell records. It's not rocket science."

Recorded in the main at Mick's home studio – where Mick produced nine of the tracks – the album also featured Wright at the forefront of work on the tracks that were seen as potential single releases including 'Perfect Love', 'Holding Back The Years' and 'Something Got Me Started'.

"If it was the days of old vinyl and you had a side one and a side two then *Simplified* would have a first side of orchestrated versions of old and new songs and on side two would be Latino versions – music from Brazil, Cuba and Jamaica – of songs.
My voice sounds much richer but I can still hit the top notes. I sounded like a seven-year-old back then but now it sounds like a record that could have been made in any era."

Working in Metropolis studios alongside Mark Jaimes and Danny Saxon, Wright's brief from the Simply Red camp was simple. "It was Ian Grenfell's idea to go to Cuba and he asked me if we could try and do some Cuban sort of tracks."

The result was that Wright sorted himself out with a selection of Cuban music and, in his own words, "re-recorded 'Holding Back The Years' with a Latin treatment and put 'Perfect Love' over a Cuban-style track."

Also on duty for *Simplified* was Hale who focussed on the non-Latin parts of the album and again he got his instructions over the phone. "Conversations with Mick were purely on a song basis. 'We've got this song and we'd like to have a string quartet on it' – end of conversation."

Even though it was going to be the summer of 2005 before he finally met up with Mick, Hale had heard that his client was a perfectionist when it came to his music. "If that's the case then it's pleasing that the only feedback I got was that he was very happy. The only thing he ever said to me was to ask if we could make a sound in a different register. I changed an octave and it was job done."

Photoshoot for *Simplified*, Fulham Town Hall, April 2005

A year after its release *Simplified* represents something of a special project for Mick and Simply Red. What started out as an unplugged album, gradually became a Latin-influenced album which, despite being a million miles away in musical style, has strong links to the latest Simply Red album entitled *Stay* which Mick describes as a "rocking soul" album.

"*Stay moved on radically from what we had planned in 2006. I wanted to go back to a style that we sort of started out with and expressed more the influences I had as a teenager, that stemmed from the Stones, The Beatles and Zeppelin. It's never been expressed in the music as much as it perhaps should have. Its not like we're turning into a rock 'n' roll band but we're bringing out a little bit more of that flavour. It's a more unified record and it's got a specific direction with melody, warmth and romance – they are love songs.*"

The new album boasts a version of Ronnie Lane's 'Debris' which featured as the B-side of The Faces' 1971 hit 'Stay With Me' and had long been a favourite with Mick.

"*It's a song I used to play in my bedroom as an old 45 single before I went to sleep. I love melancholy and I find this wonderfully romantic. I've always wanted to record it and it felt great when we put it down.*"

Also featured on the new album is a song co-written with the multi-talented Jools Holland which the band leader views as perhaps his favourite Simply Red moment. "We just sat down and wrote 'Lady' together and I have to say it is a highlight although when I travel anywhere in Europe I always hear one of his songs – either in the airport, in the taxi or in the hotel. It's like he's following me around Europe!"

Once again, Wright was alongside Mick at the production controls – and as a co-composer – on *Stay* and for the singer this partnership – which stretches back more than a decade to 1995 and 'Fairground' – represents the future as far as Simply Red's recordings are concerned.

"*It's me and Andy Wright now. He didn't come in as a producer but as a guy who was going to work with samples, but I want to co-produce with Andy now. I think he understands me and gets the music. There's a big advantage in having an independent ear and I want to give him enough space to go away and work on his ideas for Simply Red.*"

Right: Simply Red in Havana, Cuba, 2005

ACKNOWLEDGEMENTS

First and foremost the authors would like to thank all those people who made themselves available to be interviewed for this book.

Thanks also to the following people without whom this book would not have been written or published: Andy Dodd, Ian Grenfell, Elaine Gwyther, Andrea Mills, Alex Noyes and Tim Wilde at Silentway Management Ltd; Jim Greenhough, Piers Murray-Hill, and Lorna Russell at Carlton; Stuart Crouch, Melanie Hunter and Keith Peacock at Peacock.

The publishers would like to thank the following sources for their kind permission to reproduce the pictures in this book:

Richard Aujard: 137; Mark Bader: back cover, 158; Financial Times – Colin Beere: 103; Camilla Bjorvig: 3; Hamish Brown: 53, 109, 183; Paul Burns: 139 (top); Corbis Sygma – Andrew Murray: contents page/ Jacqueline Sallow 150; Paul Cox: 55, 100, 172 (top); Andy Earl: 174; Rick Guest: 177; Gusto/ Hugh Turvey: 6, 24, 52, 56, 110, 128, 144, 180, 181, 185, 188; Ian Grenfell: 135 (bottom); Elaine Gwyther: 82 (top); Bob Harding: 83 (top and bottom); London Features International – Steve Rapport 36/ Zanna 85, 161; Manchester Evening News Syndication: 14 (top), 51 (top), 96 (top and bottom); Kevin Marchant: 168; Ged Murray: 15; Fabio Nosotti: 33, 70; Margaret Pendlebury: 120 (top); Barry Plummer: 77, 157; Redferns – Stephan Engler 42; Rex Features: 134 (bottom), 149 (bottom); Rex Features – Brian Rasic 38, 39 (bottom), 72, 73, 115 (bottom)/ Andre Csillag 39 (top)/ Carl Royle 50/ Michael A Slade 97/ Sam Barcroft 120 (bottom)/ Eugene Adebari 122/ ITV 127/ News Group 135 (top)/ Richard Young 138, 140 (bottom right)/ Sipa 140 (top right); David Ralph: front cover; Sheila Rock: 59; Diane Scrimgeour: 45; Gino Sprio: 162; Dave Stoughton: 119; Richard Watt: 23; Zanna: front end-paper, 86, 88, 93, 167.

Single and album artwork reproduced by kind permission of Blood and Fire: 123; simplyred.com: 107, 176, 178, 179, 182; Warner Music UK: 69, 90, 98, 99, 147, 148, 153, 156, 160, 164, 165, 170, 171, 173.

Magazine artwork reproduced by kind permission of Music Week: 105, copyright Music Week; Viz Magazine: 126, copyright Fulchester Industries/Dennis Publishing.

Every effort has been made to acknowledge correctly and contact the source and/or copyright holder of each picture. We apologise for any unintentional errors or omissions which will be corrected in future editions of this book.

Picture Book
Money's Too Tight To Mention, *May '85*
Come To My Aid, *September '85*
Holding Back The Years, *November '85*
Jericho, *February '86*
Holding Back The Years, *June '86*
Open Up The Red Box, *August '86*

Men And Women
The Right Thing, *February '87*
Infidelity, *May '87*
Maybe Someday, *July '87*
Ev'ry Time We Say Goodbye, *November '87*
I Won't Feel Bad, *February '88*

A New Flame
It's Only Love, *January '89*
If You Don't Know Me By Now, *March '89*
A New Flame, *June '89*
You've Got It, *October '89*

Stars
Something Got Me Started, *September '91*
Stars, *November '91*
For Your Babies, *January '92*
Thrill Me, *April '92*
Your Mirror, *July '92*
Montreux EP, *November '92*

Life
Fairground, *September '95*
Remembering The First Time, *December '95*
Never Never Love, *February '96*
We're In This Together, *June '96*

Greatest Hits
Angel, *October '96*

Blue
Nightnurse, *September '97*
Say You Love Me, *May '98*
The Air That I Breathe, *August '98*
Ghetto Girl, *November '98*

Love And The Russian Winter
Ain't That A Lot Of Love, *October '99*
Your Eyes, *February '00*

It's Only Love

Home
Sunrise, *March '03*
Fake, *July '03*
You Make Me Feel Brand New, *December '03*
Home, *March '04*

Simplified
Perfect Love, *October '05*
Something Got Me Started /
A Song For You, *December '05*

Stay
Oh! What A Girl!, *September '06*

RED
TOUR '03
SIMPLY RED
A STARRY NIGHT IN
1993
VIP
SIMPLY RED
A STARRY NIGHT IN
1992
MAN
AFTER SHOW
invites you to
A Starry Night
in Central Park
with
SIMPLY RED
Reception:
where: The Boathous
when: 5:30 p.m. - 7:0
what: Drinks & Dinne
Show:
where: Summerstage
when: 7:00 p.m.
RSVP:
life
Hospitality
Simply Red hospitality pass
[No.6 Life]
SIMPLY RED
2000
THE SPIRIT OF LIFE TOUR
SIMPLY RE